MOVIE MONEY

MOVIE MONEY

2ND EDITION
REVISED AND UPDATED

Understanding Hollywood's
(Creative) Accounting Practices

BILL DANIELS, DAVID LEEDY, AND STEVEN D. SILLS

SILMAN-JAMES PRESS   LOS ANGELES

Second Edition
10 9 8 7 6 5 4 3 2 1

Library of Congress Cataloging-in-Publication Data

Daniels, Bill, 1956-
Movie money : understanding Hollywood's (creative) accounting
practices /
by Bill Daniels, David Leedy, and Steven D. Sills. — 2nd ed.
p. cm.
1. Motion picture industry—United States—Finance.
2. Motion pictures—United States--Marketing.
I. Leedy, David. II. Sills, Steven D.
III. Title.
PN1993.5.U6D25 2006   384'.830973—dc22   2005035936

ISBN: 1-879505-86-X

Cover by Lageose Design

Printed and bound in the United States of America

SILMAN-JAMES PRESS
1181 Angelo Drive
Beverly Hills, CA 90210

To my wife and true love, Cheryl Ann. To Billy and Jenny, the lights in my life. To my mother, who suffered me endlessly, and my father, who cheered me on. And to Professor Lon Sobel, who got this book off the ground.

Bill Daniels

In memory of Charles M. Powell, motion picture publicist extraordinaire and former First Vice President of the Academy of Motion Pictures Arts and Sciences, who never understood what I did for a living or how he could help, but always wanted to be my rabbi in the motion picture industry.

David Leedy

For Gail, who is my best friend. For Matt, Greg, Brad, and Jennifer, who are my joy. For my father, Gilbert Sills, CPA, who would have been proud. And to David Leedy and Bill Daniels: colleagues, co-authors, and friends.

Steven Sills

CONTENTS

FOREWORD

In 1980, I authored and self-published a booklet entitled *Motion Picture Distribution—An Accountant's Perspective.* I wrote it for several reasons: (1) I was really pissed off with the short shrift the business affairs and accounting side of the motion picture business was receiving from the press and the inability of my accounting peers to stand up for themselves; (2) since the day I got into the industry, even as an experienced Certified Public Accountant, I was continually told that I didn't understand motion picture accounting because I hadn't been around the industry long enough, and; (3) to announce to the world that I was going into business for myself as a financial consultant/CPA.

The book was a tremendous success with an enormous and favorable review by Art Murphy in *Daily Variety.* This 90-plus-page booklet, which I hand-typed (this was before home computers) on photographic paper, was used by universities all over the world. My brother-in-law, Larry Ball, a Dallas printer, printed both of my two printings. Over 5,000 copies were sold, primarily due to word-of-mouth, out of my post office box in Hollywood.

As the industry changed, many people have been after me to update my original book. Most vocal was Harold Vogel, industry analyst extraordinaire and author of *Entertainment Industry*

Economics. In 1990, I found a *real* publisher and put together a second edition, borrowing heavily from the revelations of the Art Buchwald (*Coming to America*) case. Without any of the motivation that prompted the original work and faced with a year's work polishing the new manuscript after I'd circulated the draft for comments from colleagues in the industry, I decided the incentives were just not adequate.

In 1992, Lionel Sobel, Professor of Law at Loyola Law School in Los Angeles and one of the people who had been after me for an updated version, introduced me to Bill Daniels and suggested that we collaborate. Bill is an experienced entertainment journalist and up-and-coming attorney. As my adventures in entertainment had led me away from feature films and more into the realm of colorization, animation, and special effects, I suggested a third collaborator. Steve Sills, a colleague who is terribly knowledge-able in this area and for whom I have always had the greatest respect, agreed to join with us in this project.

This final product is mostly Bill's and Steve's, although it has a base in my original work and the updated 1990 version. The criteria for this book was that it be readily understandable to industry newcomers, yet have sufficient information so as to be of value to industry veterans. Also, I wanted the book to be even-handed in its commentary regarding major motion-picture studios. I hope that we have achieved these.

David Leedy

PREFACE

Three authors are credited for this book. Steve Sills is listed last, David Leedy, before him, and then, me. In my opinion, the order is backwards, despite my best efforts to restore some order and balance to the universe. Let me explain what I mean by that.

Back in 1980, David Leedy was in private practice as a certified public accountant after a long career with Universal Pictures. As David tells it, around that time the *Los Angeles Times* was running one of its periodic exposés of Hollywood's shady accounting practices after some now-forgotten hit movie failed to earn any net profits despite obvious success at the box office. You've probably seen similar stories yourself. They generally point to a film, talk about how much money it made at the theaters, and then express astonishment and not a little outrage that a successful film hasn't ever produced a profit.

However, the proper term is *net profit*. What struck David about the *Times* story was how the reporter seemed to fall so easily into a common trap: that is, mistaking the plain vanilla profit concept with the contractually defined "net profit" term. David, in a word, was irked. So he decided to do something about it.

That something was a slender booklet titled *Motion Picture Distribution—An Accountant's Perspective*, which David wrote in 1980 and published himself. The entire printing sold out, and he still gets requests for copies.

In the early 1990s, David set about updating his book. Only, with retirement closing in, he just couldn't find the time to finish it. Even so, he circulated some early drafts for comment. One went to Lon Sobel, a prominent (now, former) Loyola Law School of Los Angeles entertainment law professor. At about that time, I was studying law under Lon after spending many years writing about the film business for *Daily Variety*. Something clicked, and Lon introduced me to David in about 1992, telling us he thought we might make good collaborators. As things turned out, he was right.

The original *Movie Money* was published in 1998 and was an immediate success. Since David had retired to a small Texas town in 1995, my name was first on the cover. I still feel a little guilty about that, because back then, I was really not much more than a student of Hollywood's creative accounting and a scribe, while David was a true master. Oh well, that's showbiz.

Anyhow, then there was Steven Sills. In those early days, Steve was reluctant to be too closely identified with this book because he was concerned it might not jibe with his very particular views on the subject matter. To understand why, you have to know Steve.

Both CPA and licensed attorney, Steve Sills was, and still is, a name partner with Sills & Adelmann, Hollywood's premier motion picture profit-participation auditing firm. You'll have to read further to fully appreciate what that means, but suffice it to say that Sills & Adelmann counts some of Hollywood's biggest stars among its extensive clientele. When it comes to unraveling Hollywood accounting, Steve Sills is the undisputed king.

He's also one of the nicest guys you'll ever want to meet. For the whole two years that I spent writing and rewriting what became *Movie Money*, Steve was my biggest resource. First, he graciously agreed to make comments on my notes, then later, when it became clear I was getting in over my head, he offered to meet me for breakfast every week, just to talk net profits. So there we sat, 8:00 a.m. every Thursday morning at Jerry's Famous Deli in Encino, talking shop for an hour before work. When I kept showing up late because I was dropping my daughter off at pre-school, Steve suggested we move our breakfast to 8:15, and then he *still* gave me a whole hour of his valuable time, week in and week out.

I showed Steve draft chapters, listened to his critiques, argued fine points of law and accounting, traded industry stories and shop talk, and fought over who is taking advantage of whom in the Hollywood struggle between talent and capital. He became a major collaborator and a close friend. We took turns picking up the check.

In the end, Steve was reluctant to take an author credit—he only accepted after my repeated begging and cajoling. In my original forward, I explained, "You see, in places, *Movie Money* doesn't adequately support his view that the net profit system is totally rigged against talent and in favor of the studios, and that bothered him in a deep and meaningful fashion. Not that Steve thinks this book shouldn't try to provide a fair perspective from both talent and studio perspectives. It's just that he can't begin to conceive that the studio view has any merit, and doesn't want anyone to be confused about that point."

Anyhow, that was 1998. Now it's 2005, the original *Movie Money* printing sold out, and our publisher, Gwen Feldman, began clamoring for an update.

Well, as it turned out, during the past seven years, Steve became more and more associated with the book, while my law practice has taken me farther and farther from the entertainment business. So I told him, Steve, buddy old pal, I'll make you a deal: You do the heavy lifting, I'll polish your prose, we'll put together a new edition, and YOU can take first position as primary author and guru. Only it didn't work out the way I planned. Our publishers kindly but firmly nixed our name-reordering scheme. Something about copyright registrations, Internet orders, confusing our readers and what-have-you. So, in the end, I still have first billing and Steve's name is last and there remains a certain disorder and lack of balance in the universe. Darn.

It remains my view that in a fair and just world, Steve Sills would be credited as the primary author of this book, David Leedy would be second and I would proudly hold forth in third position. Maybe we'll finally get it right in the third edition. In the meantime, Steve, David, know that you are and will always remain, first in my heart.

Bill Daniels

January 2006

ACKNOWLEDGMENTS

The evolution of this book owes a lot to a lot of people, many of whom we will fail to name. Please accept our apologies and our gratitude for your help.

Harold Vogel and Lionel Sobel were primary catalysts in getting this project going. Many colleagues reviewed the 1990 draft, including Frank Johnson of Price Waterhouse, Phil Cross of Coopers & Lybrand, Shadi Sanbar of Arthur Andersen, Mel Sattler, retired from MCA-Universal, and David Londoner of Wertheim Schroeder.

Special thanks to Peter Dekom, whose firm reviewed David Leedy's first book to determine if any liability might exist and who still returns Bill Daniels' telephone calls, much to Bill's continuing amazement.

To Bill's law partners, Arnie Schwartz and Marcus Bradley, two great trial lawyers who are largely responsible for keeping Bill productive and solvent. To John Williams of Vanguard Films, a great producer who appreciates backend like few others. To Ivan Axelrod, who convinced Steve Sills that he had a future in public accounting; Ben Newman and Sid Finger, who prepared Steve for that future; Bill Adelmann, Steve's former partner and current consigliere; and Michele Gentille, Steve's current partner and coworker for more than 15 years. To Jim Fox of

Silman-James Press, who made this book far better than the authors could have done by themselves, and somehow managed to keep smiling throughout the long, arduous process; and to Jim's partner, Gwen Feldman, who encouraged, challenged, and cheered the authors.

INTRODUCTION

Like any art form, motion pictures can elicit deep passion.

And like oil gushers, motion pictures can create a flood of cash.

If you work in the theatrical film business, you understand that columnist Liz Smith is understating the case when she quips about it being the toughest business in the world. You also know that success can come almost over night. If you are not prepared for success, the financial rewards can pass you right by.

Hollywood has developed a system that provides for talent and financing sources to share in the success of any given film. But like most everything in the film business, the motion picture profit-participation system is difficult to understand and arcane to apply. It's easy to speculate why this is so. One recent class-action lawsuit complains that the entire participation system amounts to nothing more than a price-fixing conspiracy by the major powers in a company town.[1] On the other hand, any number of studio executives will defend the fairness of the present system with vigor. Your own views about what is fair and what is cockeyed about motion picture profit participations will depend upon whether you side with talent or capital.

---

[1] *Garrison v. Warner Bros., Inc., et al.*, U.S. District Court, Central District of California, Case No. CV-95-8328, filed January 18, 1996.

This book's purpose is not to pass judgment on the profit participation system. That's something best left to philosophers and the courts.

Rather, this book is a tool for entertainment professionals trying to make sense of their participation deals or seeking to negotiate from knowledge. In other words, the authors are content to let others argue about what makes for a perfect world. We're more interested in explaining how you can make more money for yourself, right now.

If that's your goal, then you've come to the right place. Let's start with some ground rules.

CHAPTER ONE

THE CONTRACT LANGUAGE

Contract clauses granting profit participations can appear deceptively simple. For instance, it may be that you have a contract that promises:

- The Performer shall be entitled to contingent compensation equal to 10% of 100% of the Net Profits of the Picture.

or,

- As contingent compensation, the Purchaser shall pay the rights Owner a sum equal to 5% of 100% of the Defined Proceeds of the Picture.

Other contracts might contain much more elaborate language, such as:

- If the applicable Picture is produced and released as a live action film, contingent compensation shall be an amount equal to 20% of 100% of the Adjusted Gross Receipts (as defined below), if any, of the Picture in excess of and accruing after the Break Point (as defined below) is achieved (if ever) reducible to a soft floor of 10% of 100% of the Adjusted Gross Receipts with a hard floor of 5% of 100% of the Adjusted Gross Receipts.

Whatever the language, there's a fundamental truism that needs to be explained at the very beginning, and then highlighted, repeated, and stressed and repeated again and again. **All terms in motion picture profit participations are *defined terms*.** Never forget this.

That means that the net profits in your option contract are not the net profits that your Aunt Martha earns when she sells a 25-cent hose washer at her hardware store. For Aunt Martha, net profits are a simple affair—if the washer cost her 15 cents to stock and sell, then there is a net profit of an entire dime on the sale. In motion pictures, whether or not there is a "net profit" depends entirely upon how that term is defined in a multi-page studio definition, how many others are entitled to share in the profits—be they net, adjusted gross, pure gross, or what have you—along with where revenues are earned, when they are earned, and how they are earned.

THE BIG PICTURE

Most people probably don't think about how much of their eight-dollar movie ticket goes directly to pay the starring actor or the leading lady, never mind the director, producer, or writer. But then, of course, most people don't aspire to work in pictures.

Yet understanding how cash flows from ticket window to distributor to producer and director and star is crucial if you are to fully understand how every individual shares in the fruits of a collaborative motion picture enterprise.

It doesn't matter if you are a high-powered talent agent piecing together a difficult package deal or a production vice president negotiating for key talent. Understanding how the industry earns dollars on the one hand, and spends them on the other, is a key advantage in the rabidly competitive motion picture industry.

The wonderful thing about mastering the subtleties of motion picture participations is that, in working through the system, you can't help but develop a keen understanding about how the various players participate in each film's success or failure. That knowledge, when applied in dealmaking and sorting out deals that are already fixed, can give you an edge. It can also keep you from being edged aside when your project is a success.

In studying how the actor, the director, the writer, the producer, and even the outside financier share profits with the distributor for any given project, you come into contact with every facet of a motion picture's financial being. This is powerful knowledge.

PARTICIPATIONS = PEOPLE

Just about every modern motion picture deal allows creative talent to participate in the financial success of their collaborative efforts through profit participation. But, like most things in the motion-picture creative universe, the idea that talent can share the fruits of success with the business suits is simple only in concept.

The notion that talent should share in the success of their own creations has deep roots in Hollywood. However, it wasn't until the breakdown of the old studio system, where talent was tied up for long terms and at fixed rates, that profit participation became a widespread practice.

The generally accepted forerunner of modern motion-picture participation was the deal Lew Wasserman managed to wrangle for his client Jimmy Stewart in the early 1950s. The story goes that Universal couldn't afford Stewart's usual up-front cash fee, yet desperately wanted him to star in the upcoming feature *Winchester '73*. Wasserman solved the conundrum by obtaining a financial stake for Stewart in the success of *Winchester '73*, and when the film did well, both Stewart and Universal reaped a sizable financial benefit. In a town where everyone knows everyone else's deal, the concept quickly became entrenched.[1]

Since *Winchester '73*, the profit participation system has grown, adapted, mutated, and otherwise fought to avoid comprehension until, today, the people who actually understand how the system works are far fewer than those who use it every day. The reason has to do with the arcane manner in which power balances in Hollywood.

In modern Hollywood, six major distributors control the vast bulk of theatrical films released to the public.[2] Those same distributors also exert tremendous power and influence over what films are made, not just by providing financing, but also by providing access to the domestic theatrical marketplace (U.S. and Canadian movie theaters) in a manner that no other modern organizations can match. So, these distributors, which we will loosely refer to as "studios" for convenience's sake, not only distribute product, they are also the industry's principal bankers.

The studios have Oz-like power over the motion picture industry and cash in abundance.[3] But since the break-up of the

---

[1] Though such major players as Irving Thalberg participated in profits long before the 1950s, the Jimmy Stewart deal is generally accepted as the forerunner of the modern-day profit participation transaction.

[2] At this writing, the majors are NBC/Universal, Paramount, Sony, Warner Bros., Walt Disney and 20th Century Fox. Many of the majors also have affiliated brands: Warner is affiliated with New Line Pictures; Sony distributes under the Columbia and TriStar labels and recently purchased an interest in MGM/UA with other joint-venture partners.

[3] Or, perhaps more properly, access to abundant capital. Industry bankers and financiers regularly warn that cost structures in the motion picture industry are wildly unbalanced and threaten the long-term ability of the studios to remain viable financial enterprises. Others disbelieve any intimations that the studios are anything but cash-gushers for their corporate owners. Still, as Sony's 1995 multi-billion-dollar writedown for its Hollywood studio attests, making motion pictures remains a risky business that can consume huge amounts of cash in a short period.

studio system in the 1950s, the one element the studios don't control is creative talent. In this modern era, talent is free to make its best deal. Of course, given the limited number of studios and the relatively small number of films made each year, dealmaking doesn't exactly occur in a vacuum.

In *Road To Morocco* in 1942, Bob Hope and Bing Crosby crooned "Paramount will protect us, 'cause we're signed for five more years." That line reflected the old studio system's control over talent—even stars as big as Hope and Crosby were effectively owned and controlled by the studios that signed them. Clark Gable, for example, may be long remembered as Rhett Butler in Metro-Goldwyn-Mayer's *Gone With the Wind*, but it was a part he didn't want to play. At the time, 1939, he was under contract with MGM, which, with many strings attached, loaned him out to Selznick International Pictures.

In 2005, Julia Roberts and Will Smith look to their agents to watch after their best interests because today's stars make their deals picture by picture. The studios control distribution, but production, especially in an era where big budgets keep getting bigger, is an area where talent exercises a certain control.

Without creative talent, the power to make movies and money to finance them equal little more than a potential. Making a major motion picture takes star-power, because a star's name is perceived as something of a minimum-theater-attendance insurance policy. No one may turn out to see a newcomer's brilliant first effort, but Tom Cruise is certain to attract at least his core audience even if the film he is opening is a certifiable yawn.

Top male leads can command $20 million per picture or more. These top performers also command first-dollar gross participations, meaning that they are true partners in the upside of any given film with the distributor. The downside is solely the distributor's problem, though generally a box-office bomb will translate into a lower performance fee on a performer's next project, or at least mitigate any fee increase.

Stars aren't the only contributors to a successful film. The director plays a role, as do the writer, the producer, and the supporting cast. Capital may also play a role, with companies such as Australia's Village Roadshow contributing through joint financing. So, in this age of $65 million blockbusters that create $1 billion-plus franchises[4] of merchandise, theme-park rides, and spin-off products—George Lucas's *Star Wars* series springs to mind—talent and capital expect to share in the financial upside.

Sounds easy enough in theory. But in practice, sharing the upside takes on more shapes and permutations than the citizens of Mickey's Toontown.

---

[4] In filmed entertainment, a *franchise* refers to the continuing business opportunities that a hit motion picture generates. So, the *Batman* series is often referred to as a Warner Bros. franchise in which one hit film launched merchandising opportunities, an animated television series, and multiple sequels, with no end in sight. Other franchise properties include the *Star Trek* television shows and features and the *Star Wars* series.

PERMUTATIONS

Profit participations are calculated in terms of "points" (percentages), usually described in terms of "net" and "gross." That's about the only constant you can count on with certainty when deciphering the profit participation code.

Major stars command first-dollar gross points, which—from their name—should logically be paid from first-dollar gross revenues, but generally aren't. Less powerful contributors, such as most writers, must be content with net profit points, the variety that Eddie Murphy denigrated as "monkey points" during Art Buchwald's epic plagiarism battle with Paramount over *Coming to America*. Murphy dubbed net points in that fashion because, he quipped, they were so worthless that only a monkey would accept them. Net points sound like they logically should be paid from net profits. Yet any given contract will define "net" in a different way, and some distributors have done away with the term altogether, wary as they are after Buchwald's well-publicized courthouse victory.

There are gross points after actual breakeven, a device that is effectively a net-point substitute but which lets an agent holler on the phone, "Sweetheart, I got you GROSS!"[5]

There are soft floors and hard floors and deferments and artificial breakpoints.

---

[5] Gross points after breakeven are generally the same as net points, but without an adjustment for the distributor's distribution fee.

Sometimes the terminology seems mindnumbingly obscure, sometimes it appears quite silly. Still, at the end of the day, understanding how profit participations work can mean the difference between whether your pockets are filled with dollars . . . or holes.

FADE IN:

INT. MALIBU FASHIONABLE VILLA — DAY

SHARON SEDUCTION yawns as she opens mail over
her morning coffee. She glances quickly at
a participation statement from the studio
accounting department, then absently casts it
aside.

She reaches for her Daily Variety while
pouring a second steaming cup. Scanning
page one, Sharon's dark blue eyes lock
on a printed headline. Eyebrows furrowed,
she scans the first paragraph, then gasps
sharply. Dark brown coffee stains white table
linen. Sharon jerkily rips open her Hollywood
Reporter and feels a tightness in her chest.
She grabs the statement that a moment ago
was so carelessly tossed aside and scans the
last page as if to make sure of something.
The telephone is within reach. She snatches
the receiver from its cradle and crushes her
thumb against number one on speed dial.

                                    CUT TO:

INT. BEVERLY HILLS TALENT AGENCY

A fashionably dressed, high-powered talent
agent, MEL, swings in his comfortable leather
chair. He interrupts one telephone call to
take another. Listening a moment, he frowns
and grabs his own copy of Daily Variety.

                    MEL
          I see it. Let me make some
          calls.

                                    CUT TO:

INT. CENTURY CITY TALENT AGENCY

Two men in suits sit in leather-
upholstered chairs listening carefully.
Behind the desk is one of the firm's
top partners, VICTORIA. Her clothes are
carefully tailored to project authority,
her appearance is precise in every detail.
Of the two men, the older one, BERNIE,
sports a Humphrey Bogart painted tie over
a pristine Turnbull & Asser dress shirt.
The younger man, DAVID, wears a slightly
anxious look on his face.

                    VICTORIA
          I don't need to tell you that
          a major star like Sharon is
          extremely important to this
          firm. I want her to be happy.
          And she isn't very happy right
          now.

Bernie nods his agreement.

                    BERNIE
          I don't blame her. Power Lunch
          is a major hit because of her.
          No one denies that.

                    DAVID
          What I don't understand is how a
          film can sell $200 million worth of
          tickets and not make a profit.

                    BERNIE
               (gently)
          Net profit. The studio says it
          hasn't earned a net profit.

                    VICTORIA
          No one is pretending <u>Power Lunch</u>
          isn't a money-maker for the studio.
          What I'm concerned about is why
          Sharon isn't participating in the
          success.

                    BERNIE
          I think I can tell you that without
          even looking at the books. Two
          words: Sylvester Sturdy. I've
          been reading in the trades about
          his deal on <u>Power Lunch</u>, and even
          though the people come to see
          Sharon, the profits are going to
          Sly.

          Victoria frowns; her eyes are dark, angry
          points.

                    VICTORIA
          This firm signed off on Sharon's
          deal. If it turns out we're
          responsible for what's happening,
                    (MORE)

                    VICTORIA (cont'd)
          we could lose one of our most
          important clients.

     She points a finger at Bernie.

                    VICTORIA
          You are the motion picture
          accounting expert. I want you to
          comb through the studio books and
          tell me just what the hell is going
          on.

     She directs the same finger at David.

                    VICTORIA
          And you are going to work with
          Bernie so that this office knows
          exactly what is going on at all
          times. It won't hurt you to learn
          about profit participation, anyway.
          If we end up in litigation I'll
          need someone around here to be an
          expert on the subject.

                                   FADE OUT

BASICS

To understand why Sharon Seduction is upset, you need to understand how creative talent is compensated for its work in modern major-theatrical motion pictures.

The films Sharon appears in are what the public recognize as movies from major motion picture *studios*. The *majors,* as they are called, are actually more properly theatrical film financiers and distributors. Rather than control every intimate aspect of every film, like in the days of Jack Warner, Harry Cohn, and other legendary moguls, the majors largely content themselves with controlling the purse strings.

Of course, in this era of the mega-blockbuster, controlling the funds amounts to controlling the whole show. The average studio-financed picture in 2004 cost approximately $64 million to produce. Just to bring that film to domestic movie theaters requires another investment in prints and advertising that averaged $35 million in 2004.

A major distributor must release fifteen to twenty motion pictures each year to satisfy theater exhibitors anxious to fill empty seats. That means the minimum financial investment in each year's film slate totals in the area of $1.5 to $2 billion.

Of course, money spent does not necessarily translate into tickets sold, as the legion of well-financed interests who came to Hollywood to play in pictures and left with dramatically reshaped wallets can attest. A multi-million-dollar investment can easily evaporate if the film languishes in the can due to lack of interest. Risk is as much a part of movies as Hollywood hype and glitter.

Studios are acutely conscious about film-business risks, so they are ever on the prowl for ways to share risk. Profit participations are one way that studios can share the risk of failure with the most expensive elements that make up a motion picture—actors, writers, directors, and producers.

A sample budget from a $60 million film tells the story:

Above-The-Line

Story	$450,000
Scenario	2,175,000
Producer	1,500,000
Director	4,950,000
Principal Cast	17,505,000
Supporting Cast	1,425,000
Stunts	97,500
Fringe Benefits	1,200,000
Travel & Living	1,080,000
Above-The-Line Total	**$30,382,500**

Below-The-Line

<u>Production</u>

Extras/Stand-Ins	$795,000
Production Staff	1,470,000
Art Department	870,000
Camera	1,425,000
Set Construction	2,625,000
Miniatures	1,140,000
Set Operations	1,275,000
Electrical	1,080,000
Special Effects	270,000
Set Dressing	990,000
Props	435,000
Action Props	120,000
Wardrobe	780,000
Makeup & Hair	510,000
Production Sound	345,000
Transportation	2,100,000
Location Expense	2,550,000
Process Photography	825,000
Production Dailies	525,000
Below-the-Line Travel	1,065,000
Fringes	3,150,000
Tests	90,000
Facilities Fees	255,000
Production Total	**$24,690,000**

Post-Production

Editing	$750,000
Music	1,950,000
Post-Production Sound	645,000
Stock Shots	37,500
Titles	82,500
Opticals, Mattes, Inserts	82,500
Laboratory Processing	360,000
Fringe Benefits	120,000
Post-Production Total	**$4,027,500**

Other Direct Costs

Administrative Expense	$390,000
Insurance	300,000
Publicity	180,000
Fringe Benefits	30,000
Other Direct Costs Total	900,000
Below-The-Line Total	**$29,617,500**
TOTAL BUDGET	**$60,000,000**

In this example, above-the-line talent—the producer, writer, director, and actors—consume more than 50% of the entire production budget, even without a single dollar of deferments or profit participation.[6] Talent is, in a word, *expensive*. What's worse, from the studio's perspective, the hotter the talent, whether it be a star's box-office appeal or a producer's ability to attract star talent, the higher the cost.

That being the case, good business sense dictates that the less cash a studio needs to invest up front in any given picture, the better. Of course, it also makes sense to let talent share in a project's potential upside, since any compensation that is contingent upon success also has the added benefit of letting talent share in the risk of a flop.

What's more, the pool of individuals who qualify as bona fide "star" quality Hollywood talent at any given moment is limited to a select few, who are limited in the amount of time they are available for any given project. In other words, whatever effect supply and demand has on Tom Cruise's career, the one certainty is that if a film demands a star with Mr. Cruise's qualities and talents to be a financial success, then Mr. Cruise is in a powerful position to shape his own deal.

Players like Tom Cruise, Mel Gibson, and Julia Roberts command enough clout to demand not just huge barrels of cash

---

[6] A deferment provides for paying talent an agreed amount upon an agreed event. For example, $100,000 payable upon the first $10 million in domestic box-office gross. Profit participation, on the other hand, generally pays a percentage of calculated profit as determined by a fixed definition.

for their performances, but the opportunity to share in the revenues of a film. They are the prototypical *gross players* of filmdom.

Directors can also have enough clout to negotiate a large fee plus a gross participation. But because film directors as a class are unseen behind the camera, and hence invisible to the general public, their ability to negotiate gross deals is limited by their narrower box-office appeal.

While certain hyphenates (producer-directors) might have sufficient clout to negotiate on a par with star acting talent, a star director might more reasonably expect some sort of diluted gross participation. These come in such flavors as *Gross After CBE (cash breakeven), Post-ABE (actual breakeven) Gross, Post-Rolling ABE Gross, Gross After Artificial Break,* or *Gross From a Multiple.*[7]

As creative businesspeople on the set, established producers will often be able to participate in their own pictures on a gross basis, though they are often required to share some of their own participation dollars with other talent.

All the gross participation variants have three things in common:

- They all bear labels containing the word "gross";
- They all have something to do with a profit participation share;

---

[7] All these different varieties of "gross" describe different ways of calculating when the profit participation actually begins generating income for the participant. For example, Gross After Cash Breakeven gives the participant a gross participation after the gross receipts equal the sum of (1) defined distribution revenues, (2) a reduced distribution fee, (3) distribution expenses, (4) negative cost, (5) studio overhead, and (6) interest. Each of the other variations of gross has its own special definition. Consult the **glossary** for a more detailed explanation of each.

- They all represent financial formulas that are strict creatures of contract.

Aside from those three things, none of the variations on the gross theme has much to do with one another.

Yet, in an industry that trades on images and imagery, even the words that couch a player's compensation can have their own unique value. Just as talent has always been keenly sensitive to the size of the star on their dressing room doors, so is talent sensitive to the labels attached to their compensation deals. And while the cynical dismiss label-consciousness as frivolous vanity, the entertainment insider recognizes that being perceived as having clout is as important as actually having clout when negotiating deals.

Consider: When you belly up to the negotiation table for your next picture, would you rather arrive as a gross player like Tom Hanks or a net player whose last deal included only "monkey points?"

For the most part, writers must content themselves to be net profit participants, even though, without a script, no film would ever be made. The reason, once again, has to do with bargaining clout, and the hard fact is that few writers have the clout to demand true gross deals, though powerhouses such Michael Crichton and John Grisham are exceptions to the rule.

Actors without a following and directors without a track record are also typical net players. For them, net points are a promise of better things in the future. Today net points, tomorrow, gross!

Not that net profit participations are intrinsically worthless. Depending upon the formula used to calculate a net profit and a picture's performance in the marketplace, a net profit point can make a substantial contribution to an artist's total compensation.

But most pictures will never generate a "net profit" for the participant, even though they generate millions upon millions of dollars for the studios and others. The reason for this doesn't have anything to do with deception or bookkeeping black magic. Instead, it has everything to do with the arcane practices peculiar to the Hollywood motion picture industry.

```
FADE IN:

EXT. MELROSE BOULEVARD — DAY

A red Lamborghini races along.

Bernie is behind the wheel, zig-zagging
through the heavy traffic with quick but
fluid motions, humming a rock anthem as
if to himself. David is in the passenger
seat, holding on tightly, gritting his
teeth and trying to appear like he is
```

enjoying the ride. The convertible makes a sudden
left turn into a wide driveway, clinging to the
black asphalt like an oversized slot car. Bernie
brakes sharply at the glass kiosk, where a
uniformed guard is standing.

                    GUARD
          Good morning, Mr. Paynes.

                    BERNIE
          Good morning, Shiela.

                    GUARD
          Mr. Gallagher is expecting you. He
          left instructions for you to park
          in Lot "A."

                    BERNIE
          I know where that is. Thanks.

Bernie guides his sports car through the
motion picture studio grounds, turning into
a parking lot populated exclusively with
expensive imported automobiles. David takes
care not to scrape up against a $110,000
Mercedes coupe as he squeezes out of Bernie's
car.

                    BERNIE
          The studio is taking this
          seriously.

                    DAVID
          How can you tell?

                    BERNIE
          I've been doing audits here for
          more than fifteen years, and
          usually they make me walk from the
          far lot unless I bring bagels. Even
          then I park with the other hired
          help. It looks like our client
          commands some respect around here.
               (he grins)
          Let's keep that in mind.

                                        CUT TO:

INT. TASTEFULLY APPOINTED OFFICE — DAY

David examines an expensive modern artwork
while Bernie scribbles a note on a yellow
legal tablet. Bernie looks up to see THOMAS
GALLAGHER approaching from a hallway, and
closes his briefcase. Thomas extends his
hand with a smile.

                    THOMAS
          Good morning, Bernie. Here on
          another wild goose chase?

Bernie shakes Thomas's hand and grins
broadly.

                    BERNIE
          Nope. Just looking out for a
          struggling artist you studio guys
          are taking advantage of.

                    THOMAS
               (laughs)
          I've seen your client's humble
          mansion. I'd like to be struggling
          like her.
               (he motions)
          Come on, I've got a spare office
          you guys can use.

INT. LARGE CONFERENCE ROOM

Cartons of documents are already stacked near
a large walnut table surrounded by heavy
padded chairs. Bernie sets his briefcase
on the table and opens the top. David is
attracted to a huge plate-glass window
opening up to a spectacular view of the
entire motion picture studio lot. He draws a
breath.

                    DAVID
          You can see the whole studio from
          up here.

Bernie examines a sheet of paper in front of
him.

                    BERNIE
          You can see it from here, too.
               (he points)
          This is Sharon's participation
          statement from the studio. Come
          here. We need to get to work.

                                        FADE OUT

Sharon's profit-participation statement looks like just about any other profit-participation statement:

Power Lunch

Gross Receipts

Domestic:

Theatrical	$135,000,000
Non-Theatrical	$3,000,000
Home Video	$38,000,000
Pay/Cable Television	$15,000,000
Network Television	$13,000,000
Domestic Syndication Television	$6,000,000
Total Domestic:	**$210,000,000**

Foreign:

Theatrical	$84,900,000
Home Video	$18,600,000
Pay/Cable Television	$5,100,000
Free Television	$12,000,000
Total Foreign:	**$120,600,000**
Merchandising and Music	$3,900,000
TOTAL REVENUE:	**$334,500,000**

Expenses Chargeable To Participant

Distribution Fees	$111,000,000

Distribution Expenses:

Prints	10,000,000
Advertising	80,000,000
Taxes and Duties	9,000,000
Dues and Assessments	6,000,000
Freight, Misc.	3,000,000
Checking and Collection	3,000,000
Residuals	15,000,000
Total Dist. Exp.	**126,000,000**

Negative Cost:

Production Cost	60,000,000
Overhead	9,000,000
Interest	18,000,000
Deferments and Gross Participations	15,000,000
Total Neg. Cost:	**102,000,000**

TOTAL EXPENSES:	**$339,000,000**

Net Profit (Loss)	($4,500,000)

CREATURES OF CONTRACT

To the untrained eye, the participation statement appears fairly straightforward. Money coming in is detailed in the top section, labeled "Gross Receipts." Money going out is detailed in the bottom sections, labeled "Distribution Fees," "Distribution Expenses," and "Negative Cost." Subtract money going out from money coming in, and what's left over is the net profit available for profit participants. Simple, *n'est-ce pas?*

The problem is, understanding a participation statement isn't that easy. For example, while it is true that each item under the "Gross Receipts" heading symbolizes money flowing into the picture, the numbers do not represent ALL dollars generated by the picture from ticket sales, video rentals, etc. Rather, the numbers are pure creatures of contract. They reflect what the profit participant's contract with the studio says they reflect. Nothing more, nothing less.

Likewise, every item under "Distribution Expenses" reflects a studio accountant's interpretation of some boilerplate contract executed between talent and the studio when that particular project began. The same with the items under "Negative Cost." Production cost is not necessarily what it costs to shoot the film, but rather *what the participations contract says are costs that may be reported as "Production Cost."* The same goes for Overhead, Interest, and Deferments and Gross Participations.

The fact that *all terms in profit participation contracts and accounting are defined terms with specially defined meaning* is a critical concept to understand, but a difficult concept to grasp. If your initial impulse is to resist accepting this fundamental notion, don't think yourself unusual. Disagreements over whether terms like "net profit" can reasonably have any interpretation beyond their common commercial usage have triggered some of the most highly publicized legal battles the film industry has ever encountered.

For instance, when humorist Art Buchwald litigated against Paramount Pictures in 1990 for a percentage of the Eddie Murphy blockbuster *Coming To America*, the biggest fight wasn't over whether or not the picture was plagiarized from an idea sold to the studio by Buchwald and his partner, Alain Bernheim.

No. The biggest guns thundered over each side's notion of what the term "net profits" meant to a motion picture profit participant. Buchwald argued furiously that net profits in the motion picture industry should mean exactly the same thing as it does in the widget business, i.e., you sell the widgets, deduct expenses, and what's left over is the net profit.

Paramount argued just as ardently that net profits in a motion picture participation context is a *defined term* that has no meaning other than that contained in the lengthy participation contract that Buchwald and Bernheim signed with the studio.

The trial judge in Art Buchwald's case sided with the humorist, and awarded damages. But in a similar legal brawl involving the megahit *Batman*, a trial judge reached precisely the opposite result, and refused to rewrite the participations contract defining precisely how and when *Batman* would generate net profits.[8]

Which side is right? The winning side, of course. This is the second important lesson to be learned about how money flows in motion pictures.

For all its corporate trappings, the film industry remains a wild and woolly entrepreneurial frontier. In an industry where major assets such as Steven Spielberg, Mel Gibson, and Nicole Kidman walk about on two feet, and where a $100 million investment fits neatly into a half dozen 70-millimeter film cans, the deal is the thing. And since the days of handshake deals are long past, it pays to read the contract carefully.

---

[8] The case, *Batfilm Productions, Inc., et al. v. Warner Bros., Inc., et al.,* is discussed in a later chapter.

Chapter Two

THIS THING CALLED "GROSS"

Participation statements tell a story about a film from a financial perspective. Each of the lines on the statement represents a mini-industry within the larger motion picture business. Everything from U.S. movie theaters to British video sales is included on the statement. But it takes a trained eye to understand the meaning behind the words and numbers.

When Sharon Seduction reviews her profit participation statement, she always begins by examining the section labeled "Gross Receipts." This section is broken up into two main subsections. The first is labeled "Domestic" and reflects funds earned in the U.S. and Canada. The second, which bears the simple tag "Foreign," reports revenue from the rest of the known universe.

Within each of these two headings are subheadings that list revenues from various discrete market segments, such as theatrical distribution, home video, and pay-television.

The revenue is totaled. The studio then deducts a distribution fee and various costs that are itemized at length.

At the very bottom line is a final number representing either a defined profit or loss. That is the number used to determine whether or not a participant is entitled to share in any profits.

```
FADE IN:

INT. TASTEFULLY APPOINTED OFFICE — DAY

The same as before. Bernie points at the
paper in front of him.

                    BERNIE
          These line items on this
          participation statement aren't
          just numbers and headings. Each
          of them represents a different
          facet of the major motion picture
          industry.

He rises from his chair and gestures toward
the plate-glass windows on the far wall.
```

                    BERNIE
          It's just like the view through
          each of those windows. Over there
                    (he points toward
                    one window)
          are the soundstages where the pro-
          duction people work. Then over
          there . . .
                    (he points at another)
          . . . is where the studio does
          its distribution to domestic movie
          theaters.
                    (he motions in other
                    directions)
          Those are the television distribu-
          tion quarters. Home video is over
          that way, foreign distribution
          works out of those offices, the
          music and merchandising people are
          over there.

          Bernie sits back in his chair, gazing out
          at the blue sky.

                    BERNIE
          Have you ever heard the term
          "distribution windows?"

          David nods. Bernie motions to the wall of
          window glass and laughs.

                    BERNIE
          Maybe these are what people are
          talking about.

                                        FADE OUT

MARKET SEGMENTS

Theatrical revenues reflect the distributor's share of every dollar generated by movie-theater ticket sales. This number is always listed first, and not out of nostalgia for the era when theaters were the only market for theatrical films. The fact is, even though we live in a world saturated by home video, cable television, and various new media, theatrical exhibition remains the key market for motion pictures. To understand how a film relates to the various markets, picture a locomotive pulling a long train. Theatrical exhibition is the diesel engine. All other markets follow along like dutiful boxcars.

Theatrical exhibition is the major factor in persuading the public what they want to see, even if that public never sets foot inside a motion picture theater. And how well and how long a picture plays in theaters has everything to do with its value in other markets.

The reasons are various and sundry. Theatrical play creates name awareness and excitement—that "buzz" the media likes to write about. The initial advertising campaigns are generally enormous and well-funded. Every hometown newspaper has a film critic who touts the latest releases. People talk film at parties and page through the movie section while planning their weekends. Teenagers pick through the movie listings to plan the perfect date.

Following theatrical revenue on a participation statement is always non-theatrical revenue. This is a generally a small-ticket item derived from varied and diverse sources. Today, the largest single non-theatrical revenue source is the airlines. But this number also includes public exhibition licenses to military bases, prisons, oil companies, hospitals, schools, college campuses, public libraries, railroads, and churches.

Home video revenues come from the sale of DVDs and videocassettes to wholesalers and retailers. Periodically, studios and video retailers, such as Blockbuster and Hollywood Video, enter into revenue-sharing arrangements where units are sold to the retailers at a reduced rate and the studios share in the rental revenue.

Next are pay/cable television revenues earned from licenses paid by pay-TV programmers such as Time Warner's Home Box Office and Viacom's Showtime. These license fees might be paid on individual titles or be pre-negotiated for an entire range of titles in an "output deal."[1]

Network television revenues come from licenses sold to national broadcast networks. During the 1980s, when pay-TV was in rapid ascent, network revenues for theatrical films were just about nil. Today, the television networks are back in the film business, and the participation statements reflect that market swing.

Domestic syndication television tracks revenues from licenses sold to basic cable stations or individual stations across the

---

[1] An *output deal* is a contract that gives a pay programmer exclusive rights to the output of a given supplier for a set period. So, Home Box Office might make an output deal with Paramount for all of that studio's theatrical pictures for a multiple-year period. During the terms of the deal, Home Box Office must pay Paramount a fee for each of its releases, and Paramount cannot license its pictures to any other pay service.

U.S. and in Canada. In the syndication market, films are sold to stations in packages of ten, twenty, or more. As you will discover later, this practice creates some interesting questions for the participant because Hollywood has its own unique way of allocating license fees to each film in the package.

On the foreign side, the primary markets—theatrical, home video, pay/cable TV, and free-TV—are all accounted for. Foreign markets grow in importance with each passing year and, for a growing number of films, make the difference between a money-losing picture and money in the bank.

The last line on the revenue list is merchandising and music. This item covers revenue from licensing such products as lunch-pails and T-shirts, sales of soundtrack records, and so forth. Depending upon the type of film, this number might be nominal. On the other hand, merchandising for pictures such as *Star Wars* or *Shrek* can represent a huge bonanza, while *Grease* was a music soundtrack monster.

Films are exploited in a different manner in each market segment. The business customs and practices in the domestic theatrical market are quite different from those in foreign theatrical. Home video revenues flow differently from pay-TV license funds. Network broadcasting speaks a different language than syndicated television. The only consistent rule is that there is no consistency from market to market.

Even so, the various market segments do interact in how they contribute to raising public demand for any given motion picture. In Sharon Seduction's case, *Power Lunch* was a huge domestic theatrical hit, generating more than $275 million in ticket sales. A hit theatrical film becomes a cultural phenomenon of sorts. Starting before and continuing through its theatrical run, a hit film generates high levels of almost brand-name awareness with the moviegoing public. Typically, a hit attracts tons of publicity from newspapers, magazines, and television shows. The studio will try to exploit this media feeding frenzy by significantly increasing the dollars spent on television, radio, and print advertising.

Each week *Power Lunch* played in theaters, the public had another week to come into contact with the film, either directly by buying a ticket or indirectly by word of mouth or by reading about it in the press.

When the film arrived on store shelves as a DVD, there was a built-in demand. By the time *Power Lunch* hit the pay-TV market, it was a well-known commodity, prompting HBO to play it as many times each week as their contract permitted.[2]

Power Lunch was such a big hit with the public that a major broadcast network decided to pay a hefty fee for a license to show it, bringing even more money into the till. By the time the network was done, the picture was considered a classic. After the studio tied it with nine lesser-known titles in a syndicated TV package, it not only sold itself, but it helped other, more marginal, films earn extra income from that market.

The *Power Lunch* craze triggered a healthy sale of T-shirts bearing Sharon Seduction in a sexy pose. And with teenage boys

---

[2] The contract will generally permit a fixed number of showings within a fixed time period, e.g., 15 runs over 3 days.

around the world plunking down twenty bucks for a life-sized Sharon Seduction stand-up poster, merchandising revenues were substantial.

So it's understandable why Sharon Seduction hit the proverbial ceiling when the motion picture trade publications *Daily Variety* and *The Hollywood Reporter* reported that *Power Lunch* had grossed $275 million at the box office, qualifying it as one of the season's biggest smashes.

Sharon didn't make it to the pinnacle of stardom by being stupid. She recognizes that the $135 million reported on her statement as domestic theatrical gross receipts is nowhere near the number reported in the "trades." She also understands that, as a profit player, the numbers on her statement aren't abstractions, they reflect whether she will be able to buy that small Vermont town she's been eyeing, or have to settle for something less.

She's been around long enough to know that the studio looks after its own interests, and only Sharon looks after Sharon's interests.

DOMESTIC THEATRICAL

Ticket Dollars

Have you ever wondered what percentage of your theater ticket money went to pay Brad Pitt or Sandra Bullock?

You'll recall that Sharon Seduction read in the "trades" that *Power Lunch* collected more than $275 million at the box office. But when she looked at her profit participation statement, it reported receipts from domestic theatrical at a mere $135 million. Having heard about how studios regularly cheat talent with fancy bookkeeping, Sharon naturally became concerned.

What Sharon doesn't know is that the film grosses reported every Tuesday in the "trades" represent the *estimated* amount of box-office receipts, nothing more and nothing less. Due to the varied and sundry terms between distributors on the one hand and theater owners (known as "exhibitors") on the other, box-office receipts generally range between two or three times the amount paid as a license fee. On average, the license fee for major studios is 40% to 45% of the total box office. Heavy hits will command a 50% license fee, and major smashes may rise as high as 55%. Smaller distributors typically command smaller license fees falling in the 33% range. That number reflects the typical independent's lack of bargaining leverage, which in turn is due to their inability to provide a steady stream of product to exhibitors.

In other words, when the participation statement reports *Gross Receipts: Domestic: Theatrical*, that number represents film rentals, i.e., the fee paid by the exhibitor to the distributor. The statement does *not* report *gross sales*, i.e., the total ticket sales generated by the picture.

Every distributor has boilerplate language in its participations contracts that spells out precisely what it means by the term "film rental." For example, in some of its contracts, Walt Disney Pictures has defined film rental as:

> Amounts received by [Walt Disney Pictures] for the license or privilege to exhibit the picture in any and all motion picture media including theatrical, free-TV, non-theatrical exhibitions, cable or pay-TV, videocassette or other audio-visual device and any other motion picture media, whether now known or hereafter devised, but excluding amounts received from flat sales, advance payments, or security deposits (unless earned by exhibition or broadcast or forfeited), and refunds, rebates, or adjustments granted other persons by [Disney].

Aside from being a world-class run-on sentence, the Disney definition distinguishes itself by including *everything* that could possibly be earned by licensing a film into the "film rental" term.

In Sharon Seduction's case, the number she read in the trades was *theatrical film grosses*, representing total ticket sales. The smaller number on her participation statement was *theatrical film rental*, or how much the exhibitor paid the studio for the privilege of exhibiting *Power Lunch*. Film rental is always a fraction of total ticket sales.

But understanding the difference between grosses and rental does not mean Sharon can breathe a sigh of relief and relax on her porch. Understanding the terminology is only the first step in determining whether the dollars reported are fair, or even correct.

Theatrical Film Rental

Theatrical film rental is negotiated and computed in a variety of ways. The fact that the formula is never constant reflects a consistent truth: The distributor will always try to maximize film rental receipts, and the exhibitor will always attempt to keep as many ticket-sale dollars as possible.

For every individual picture, there is an exhibition contract for each theater where that film will play, signed by both the distributor and the exhibitor.[3] The contract spells out the period of time the film will play at the exhibitor's theaters. It specifies the amounts devoted to advertising support and how ad costs will be shared. Finally, it declares precisely how film rental is to be computed for the course of the engagement.

Aside from terms requiring the exhibitor to pay a minimum guarantee for any particular picture, film rental is seldom computed

---

[3] Interestingly enough, there is an individual contract for each theater, even when the distributor makes its deal with an exhibition chain with hundreds of screens.

at a flat rate for a first-run motion picture.[4] The most common arrangement is a revenue split between distributor and exhibitor, i.e., a 90/10 split with 90% of revenues going to the distributor and 10% to the exhibitor (see the example that follows).

These arrangements usually provide a minimum percentage for the distributor, an amount called a "floor," regardless of any fixed "house allowance." In theory, the floor is the absolute minimum share of ticket sales that will flow into the distributor's pocket.

The floor percentage is usually diminished by a set amount each week the picture remains at any particular venue. In week one, the deal might be a 90/10 split with a 70% floor, in week two 90/10 with a 60% floor, week three 90/10 with a 50% floor, etc.

The exhibition agreement will also generally guarantee the exhibitor a "house allowance" or "house nut," an amount whose supposed purpose is to reimburse the theater owner for the cost of opening his doors. In reality, the house nut is simply a contractual figure that is negotiated for each film. An exhibitor with clout can usually negotiate a house nut that not only guarantees it will cover its costs, but will also provide a modest profit. Needless to say, some powerful exhibitors have enough clout to demand, and receive, better terms than others with less bargaining leverage.

For the record, the *real* money in exhibition is not admissions, it's concession sales. Popcorn, soda, and gummy bears are

---

[4] However, it is worth noting that a flat rate is not uncommon in subsequent runs, should the film remain in theaters past its initial run.

where exhibitors make their real dough. None of that income flows to the profit participant. Theater owners keep 100% of their concession profits, and that is unlikely to change at any time in the foreseeable future.[5]

In the case of *Power Lunch*, the studio distributor negotiated a standard agreement that looked like this:

Negotiated House Allowance ("House Nut") = $10,000/week

Week # 1 90/10 split with a 70% floor

Week # 2 90/10 split with a 60% floor

Week # 3 90/10 split with a 50% floor

Week # 4 90/10 split with a 40% floor

Week # 5 90/10 split with a 35% floor

Weeks # 6 through infinity, same as week #5

At the Silver Screen theater circuit, *Power Lunch* sold $40,000 in tickets during each of its two weeks. Under the agreement, the dollars were divided as follows:

Week # 1

90/10 = 90% x ($40,000 - $10,000)   = $27,000

Floor = 70% x $40,000   = $28,000

Week # 2

90/10 = 90% x ($40,000 - $10,000)   = $27,000

Floor = 60% x $40,000   = $24,000

---

[5] This is even though several major exhibition chains are owned or controlled by studios.

In each case, the distributor is contractually entitled to collect whichever total is the largest, since the "floor" acts to impose a minimum on the amount payable to the distributor.

So, in Week # 1, the distributor is entitled to receive $28,000 in film rental, since the floor amount is greater than the distributor's 90% split, minus the house nut. In Week # 2, the result is exactly the reverse. The distributor's 90% minus the house nut is $27,000, an amount greater than the 60% floor. So the distributor is entitled to $27,000.

It goes without saying that regardless of the floor amount, the exhibitor retains 10% of the split revenues each week, in addition to whatever portion of its house nut it can collect. Add in popcorn sales, and exhibition can be a very nice business.

Of course, exhibitors with clout expect premium terms, and they get them. By virtue of their size and market dominance, they can command substantially better terms than the standard 90/10 split with a 70% floor arrangement.

Obviously, using a split arrangement with a floor and a house nut, it is to the exhibitor's advantage to keep a film playing as many weeks as possible. The modern multiplex theater operation is perfectly suited to keeping films on the big screens for the maximum number of weeks, since a picture can be opened in a large room, and can then be moved to smaller and smaller rooms as the weeks pass and interest begins to wane.

There are special cases in which large, single-screen theaters do thrive, however. In midtown Manhattan, the Loop in Chicago, and Westwood in Los Angeles, prestigious single-screen theaters thrive as special venues for launching a new film into the market. These prestige venues often command terms that nearly amount to giveaways by the distributors because of the high visibility these special venues command. Opening a film in these venues adds to the public's perception of a film's opening as an "event" and helps bolster awareness of the picture. In these select cases, screening a picture at a special venue is almost akin to advertising.

Cash Versus Accrual Accounting

At this point, it's necessary to discuss a burning question in profit participations: Is the normal studio practice of reporting motion picture revenue *when collected* and expenses *when incurred* fair to all concerned, or is this just another clever mechanism that Hollywood uses to cheat on its obligations? In all other industries, accountants choose either cash or accrual accounting when reporting their numbers. Only in the film industry will an accountant tell you with a straight face that not only can the two be used together, it makes good sense to do so.

Accounting terminology aside, the issue about when revenue is recognized versus when expenses are booked has important significance to the profit participant on the one hand and to the studio on the other. But first, just what this discussion is all about requires a little explaining.

The normal accounting practice in motion pictures is to only report revenue when the dollars are collected. Financial professionals know this as cash accounting.[6] (If you aren't a financial professional, it's still cash accounting.)

But not so with the expenses incurred while creating and releasing a major motion picture. Those expenses are booked the moment they arise, whether or not the studio has actually sent out a check. This is known as accrual accounting.[7]

One of the basic principals in accounting for just about every industry *except* filmed entertainment is that someone initially chooses whether to account by cash or accrual, and once that choice is made, that's how the accounting is performed forever after.

However, the motion picture industry is populated with many bright, creative people. So it was probably inevitable that in profit participation, cash and accrual accounting is mixed in the same set of books as a normal matter of course.[8]

Even though this practice is sometimes criticized as overly creative to the point of near fraud, from a distributor's standpoint, mixing cash and accrual accounting is not deceptive nor unfair, but simply necessary.

The nature of the business requires that money gets paid out in regular parcels, but flows back to the coffers in dribs and drabs.

For example, a distributor must commit certain numbers of dollars for cooperative advertising. Those funds are paid out as

---

[6] *Cash Accounting* is an accounting method in which revenue is recognized when cash is received and expenses are recognized when cash is distributed.

[7] *Accrual Accounting* is an accounting method in which revenue is recognized when earned and expenses are recognized when accrued.

[8] These accounts are kept solely for profit participation reporting. More conventional reporting is utilized for such purposes as tax accounting. Hence the oft-repeated notion that Hollywood studios keep multiple sets of books for the same picture.

a film is being released in theaters, and represent real dollars being paid for current services.

On the other hand, when it comes to the exhibitor paying film rental, the cash doesn't flow quite as quickly. Knowing that money departs easily but arrives erratically creates a dilemma for the studio in calculating profits for participants. If the studio chooses pure cash accounting, then it may well overpay the participant, since some expenses won't be billed until long after they are incurred.

For example:

PURE CASH ACCOUNTING
January 1, 2006

Film Rental	$10,000
Distribution Fee @ 30%	$3,000
Expenses Paid	$5,000
Net Profit (Loss)	$2,000

Net profit due to participants = $2,000

February 1, 2006

Film Rental	$10,000
Distribution Fee @ 30%	$3,000
Expenses	
Paid by January 1, 1997	$5,000
Paid after January 1, 1997	$3,000
Net Profit (Loss)	($1,000)

Net profit due to participant = $0

Under this scenario, if the studio paid $2,000 to the profit participants in January, then it will be billing those same participants for refunds in February. Not only is this an administrative burden, but ask yourself honestly, if you got a $2,000 check in January, are you going to pay it back in February when you don't have any other business with that studio, your checking account is fluctuating downward, and the money has been gone so long you can't recall exactly what you spent it on?

So, pure cash accounting is problematic from the studio's point of view in accounting for theatrical receipts and expenses.

On the other hand, pure accrual accounting has hazards for the profit participant. For example:

	ACCRUAL	CASH
Film Rental Due	$10,000	$10,000
Uncollected Rental	n/a	($10,000)
Reported to Participant	$10,000	-0-
Distribution Fees @ 30%	$3,000	-0-
Bad Debts	$10,000	n/a
Loss to the Picture	($3,000)	-0-

Of course, from the participant's view, when film rental is not reported until collected while advertising expenses are reported as incurred, the effect is to reduce the revenues flowing in from markets that might be paying more quickly and reliably than the theatrical market.

Frankly, this is an area where the authors still debate whether or not the current Hollywood practice is fair or fraudulent. Maybe someone will decide the issue once and for all someday, or perhaps it will always remain an area of controversy.

Oh to live in a perfect world.

FOREIGN THEATRICAL

FOREIGN FILM RENTAL

Once upon a time, domestic box-office was indisputably the single dominant factor in the film business. But the global markets grew steadily until, in 1994, for the first time, international theatrical revenues outshone the domestic box-office 52% to 48%.[9] Today, pictures can generate as much as 60% of their theatrical revenues from foreign distribution. In the modern film business, a picture no longer needs to be successful in domestic theaters to be a financial success.

As a profit participant, understanding how revenues are gathered in the foreign theatrical markets is complicated by the fact that studios must use different distribution methods to

---

[9] Claudia Eller, "Average Cost of Making, Marketing Movie Soars," *Los Angeles Times*, March 8, 1995. The MPAA (Motion Picture Association of America) reported that in, 1994, the foreign marketplace accounted for 41% of all film revenues, including theatrical, video, and television.

exploit the overseas territories than they do in the U.S., where each studio simply maintains a single, integrated distribution structure.[10] Even so, some broad generalities apply.

For the most part, the major distributors distribute their pictures in foreign markets either by utilizing their own foreign subsidiaries, by employing a foreign affiliate, or by engaging a subdistributor. As a general rule, the distributors report foreign film rentals to profit participants when the rental is actually collected from the foreign distributor. What a studio reports as revenue from foreign markets, however, isn't always equivalent to what it actually collects in cash from its foreign affiliate or subdistributor.

The studio will generally report to the participant 100% of the film rental received by the foreign distributor (be it affiliate or independent subdistributor) as revenue. It does so even though the foreign distributor seldom forwards 100% of film rentals to the studio. The resulting amount reported as revenue is generally larger than the amount the studio receives in cash. However, in reporting a larger number, the studio is entitled to charge a larger distribution fee than if only cash receipts were reported.

The studio actually receives less than 100% of the foreign film rentals because of the expenses attached to distributing pictures abroad. The foreign distributor will deduct its own distribution fees and expenses from any film rentals to reimburse itself for its own costs and to generate a profit. In addition, there may be

---

[10] At various times in film history, small independent domestic distributors have handled specialty films or sold into niche markets. However, at this juncture, the large studios dominate domestic distribution, and only a select few independents can truly offer themselves as alternatives to the majors.

remittance or withholding taxes on any funds actually remitted, or qualifying to be remitted, to the United States.

Even so, the studio reports 100% of the total film rental received by the foreign distributor to net profit participants and then uses that figure in calculating its own distribution fee.

The lesson: Some calculations seem contrived because they are. As studio participation definitions have evolved, some ways of calculating profit and expenses seem to have lost their logical moorings and appear to be defensible only because they are one small element in a greater profit equation.

Studios defend these stilted definitions and practices by arguing that, ultimately, they need to earn a certain return on their investment no matter how they reach that number. So odd practices, such as reporting 100% of foreign revenue and charging a full distribution fee on that number even though cash in pocket is significantly less, serve a functional purpose for the studio—and create an area of dispute for participants.

This doesn't necessarily mean that a peculiar calculation necessarily will reach an unfair result. However, it is a good idea to pay attention to how any given profit calculation operates, no matter which side of the transaction you are on.

Foreign Agency Sales

The major studios generally have extensive foreign-distribution systems in place to service their steady year-round motion picture output. Even so, there are alternatives to the majors in foreign markets that have no domestic equivalent.

That gives rise to a certain freedom for those wishing to bypass the majors when exploiting offshore territories. So, independent producers and financiers will often pre-sell their films to foreign distributors through foreign sales agents, even if they distribute domestically through a major studio.

Foreign sales agents are a rough-and-tumble entrepreneurial group that acts as go-betweens between film producers and foreign distributors. As go-betweens, sales agents fulfill an invaluable role, since a producer will seldom maintain relationships with distributors in any of the several hundred national marketplaces that make up the various foreign territories.

For their part, any given distributor in a foreign territory is unlikely to have sufficient resources to maintain a constant presence in the United States in order to gain access to desirable motion picture titles. Foreign sales agents bridge the gap.

Sales agents and foreign distributors typically gather each year at three major film markets: the Mifed market in Milan, Italy; the Cannes market in the South of France, held in conjunction with the Cannes Film Festival; and the American Film Market in Santa Monica, California. To add strength to their numbers, the sales agents are banded together through their own trade group, the American Film Marketing Association (AFMA).

AFMA provides innumerable invaluable services for its members, such as preparing annual credit reports on foreign distributors so that sales agents can separate the substantial from the shady. The AFMA organization also has helped bring order to what would otherwise be an unorganized distribution mish-mash.

As part of this effort, AFMA developed a distribution agreement form that provides standardization for agency sales. Of special interest to profit participants is how the standard distribution agreement requires payment. Under the agreement, payments from distributors are due when each of five key events occurs:

(1) On execution of the presell agreement;

(2) On commencement of principal photography;

(3) On completion of principal photography;

(4) On first notice that the picture can be delivered;

(5) On later dates, such as when the picture is actually delivered, after the picture's release in the foreign territory, etc.

After a sales agent has sold a title to a foreign distributor, he will generally require that the distributor either put a guaranteed amount of cash into an escrow account or obtain an irrevocable letter of credit from an acceptable bank.

Since rights that are presold in foreign territories can actually generate cash or bankable receivables prior to a film's production, presale agreements are used by some producers as a means of production financing. Where a picture is in a position to command strong presales before the first camera rolls, such as star vehicles for such bankable exports as Tom Cruise, presales help spread financial risk among numerous foreign distributors.

It isn't unusual for presale advances to consist of an initial cash payment plus a minimum guarantee. The cash is immediately available to the producer, while the remaining portion of the guarantee may be pledged as collateral to obtain a production loan.

In addition to limiting a producer's financial exposure in any given project, presale agreements will generally provide the producer a specified percentage of any film rentals earned after the foreign distributor has recouped its own investment.

Foreign distributors usually retain a distribution fee computed from the first dollar of film rental. The distributor will recoup its guarantee and distribution costs before any additional amounts, known as "overages," are payable to the sales agent, and hence the producer.

From an accounting perspective, a foreign distributor's report comparing the results before it recoups its guarantee and distribution expenses and after it has fully recouped the guarantee and distribution expenses might look like this:

	Example #1 Before Recoupment	Example #2 After Recoupment
Film Rental	$200,000	$500,000
Deductions:		
Distribution Fee @ 40%	$80,000	$200,000
Distribution Expenses	$75,000	$125,000
Guarantee	$100,000	$100,000
Total Deductions	$255,000	$425,000
(Unrecouped)/Overage	($55,000)	$75,000

The foreign sales agent might then report to the producer/ financier or other participant as follows:

	Example #1 Before Recoupment	Example #2 After Recoupment
Guarantee	$100,000	$100,000
Overage	n/a	$75,000
Total	$100,000	$175,000
Sales Agent Fee @ 20%	$20,000	$35,000
Net Amount Payable to Participant	$80,000	$140,000

From the profit participant's perspective, the way a foreign sales agent accounts for foreign film rentals offers benefits that aren't available through the major distributors.

True, there is a sales agent fee that the majors do not charge. But that is offset by the fact that the participants get their share of the film rental guarantee before the picture has earned film rental in excess of deductions.

In Example #1, a participant in a film distributed through a major would receive nothing from foreign distribution and the unrecouped $55,000 would offset any positive amounts earned in other markets for the same picture, such as domestic theatrical or home video. That isn't the case where a sales agent has presold a film. So using a sales agent allows for separating distribution results from different market areas, while distributing through the majors results in offsetting each market segment against the other, a practice known as market "cross-collateralization."

On the other hand, the sales agent fee acts to limit the upside from foreign markets should a picture prove to be a tremendous hit. And it may be that cross-collaterialization is not a problem where a film is so strong that it earns profits in every market segment.

NON-THEATRICAL FILM RENTAL

Non-theatrical film-rental revenue is generated by public-performance licenses sold to venues that aren't regular theatrical motion picture theaters.

The term "non-theatrical" is defined in the Paramount Pictures Corporation Net Profit Definition - Exhibit "A" (version 7/5/80) at page 20, Paragraph VIII.A.(2):

> Non-Theatrical
>
> Non-Theatrical exhibition means exhibition in 16mm, 35mm gauge, or lower in or by schools, hospitals, college campuses, prisons, individuals, oil companies, public libraries, railroads, private institutions, social clubs, churches, and similar usages excluding theatrical exhibitions.

The primary non-theatrical market is the airlines, which license in-flight movies. The military is also a key non-theatrical market, and remains listed in this fashion even though the familiar image, as captured in *M*A*S*H*, of the 16mm projector showing a film for the camp has given way to the modern 35mm base motion-picture theater. Other important non-theatrical markets are prisons, oil companies, hospitals, and schools.

The non-theatrical license fee is usually a flat negotiated price, or an agreed amount per viewer. As Sharon Seduction's profit statement shows, non-theatrical licenses are generally a minor portion of a film's total revenue.

HOME VIDEO

Home video distribution started out by selling funny little plastic boxes with magnetic tape in them. For many years, videocassettes were distributed using one of two distinct sales formats: rental or sell-through. Rental units were priced for the retail market at $80-$100 with a wholesale price equal to 60% of retail. Sell-through units were priced at $20-$30 for the retail market. The decision as to which sales format to choose depended upon whether the studio believed the title was one its customers would want to view just once and return (rental) or add to their home library (sell-through).

With technological advancements, the motion picture industry shifted to Digital Video Disc (DVD) format. Pricing was stabilized and the standard wholesale pricing leveled out at $13-$15. Although there is still a rental market for DVD, the retailers pay the same price for those units they rent and those that they sell. Videocassettes own an ever-decreasing share of the market and appear to be bound for extinction.

The home video market (i.e., DVDs and videocassettes) is a huge market. How big is it? Large enough that it is common for gross video sales to equal or exceed gross theatrical revenues.

Even so, Sharon Seduction's profit statement reports only $38 million from domestic home video and $18.6 million from foreign, substantial fractions of the $135 million domestic theatrical rentals and $84.9 million foreign theatrical rentals. What's going on here?

The answer requires telling one of the Hollywood film industry's most tangled tales. It's also a lesson in how profit participation calculations can take on a life of their own.

The 20% Royalty

Only one number has any serious meaning for the profit participant: 20%. That's because, with the exception of "A" level talent with negotiating leverage, the standard participation statement generated by every filmed entertainment company reports home video revenue as a standard 20% royalty on wholesale sales. The reason for this practice is rooted in history. The studios will claim that the percentage remains fixed by practical necessity.

In the 1970s, Sony Corporation began marketing videocassette recorders. The Betamax, as it was known, was sold purely as an off-television recording device for a practice known as "time-shifting." Owners of the Betamax could record a program on television while they were at work and watch it later that evening when they got home. With the exception of certain pornographic materials, there was nothing in the way of prerecorded filmed entertainment available for Betamax owners in those early days.

In time, an American entrepreneur, Andre Blay, saw other uses for the videocassette player. He formed a company called Magnetic Video and began negotiating with 20th Century Fox to license their feature-film library so that Fox titles could become available to Betamax owners in their homes. During a lengthy series of negotiations, the two sides weighed hardware marketing costs, software manufacturing, packaging, marketing and distribution, and calculated a reasonable profit for Magnetic Video. With all those costs in mind, and figuring in risk commensurate with starting a new industry—the home video industry—from scratch, the parties agreed that Magnetic Video would pay Fox a 20% royalty.

The number took on a Talmudic quality. Soon, all of the studios adopted the 20% of wholesale royalty as the inter-company rate their captive home-video companies would pay their film-licensing companies, and the number that in turn would be reported to profit participants. Contracts were rewritten to define home video revenue as those amounts received by the parent company only. When this language proved too vague, the contracts were rewritten again to limit reportable home-video revenue to 20% of wholesale, regardless of which entity received the revenue.[11]

The reason the studios retained a standard 20% was three-fold. First, they did it because they could. Second, contracts with "most favored nations" provisions were prevalent in the industry, requiring the studios to pay their highest royalty to all

---

[11] Even so, in the early years, there were deals in excess of the standard rate by non-major distributors. Specialty video distributors such as Media Home Entertainment paid substantial advances for home-video distribution rights, usually the equivalent of a 50% royalty on the wholesale price. However, as video became more important, eventually equaling theatrical distribution in gross retail revenue, the majors refused to accept independent films for theatrical distribution without home video rights attached. The independents found themselves limited to art films and "B" titles, and their role diminished accordingly.

those whose contracts contained the "most favored nations" clause.[12] So, giving anyone a better deal on home video revenue meant tremendous exposure because it automatically ratcheted up the amount due under sundry other contracts.[13]

Lastly, the studios were concerned about the powerful Hollywood guilds.

As will be discussed later in greater detail, Hollywood has developed an elaborate mechanism to compensate talent when films are utilized beyond their primary markets, i.e., theatrical distribution. "Residuals" are commonly paid whenever a film is exploited in a secondary market, such as broadcast or pay-TV. Clearly, home video is also a secondary market requiring residual payments.

Just as Fox paid residuals on the 20% royalty it received from Magnetic Video, and later from Magnetic Video's successor company, CBS/Fox Video, all of the studios limited their residual payments to the 20% royalty they received from their captive companies. It's easy to conclude that a powerful motivator was that a higher payment to anyone else would have aroused suspicion at the unions.

---

[12] A "most favored nations" clause is a standard ego provision in Hollywood contracts that basically states, "If anyone else ever gets a better deal, then I get that same better deal."

[13] The studios did not restrict the 20% rate to new agreements. Typically in the early days, even existing participants with contracts dating before home video were paid the "standard" rate. This, even though their agreements provided for revenue from the distributor, its agents, affiliates, subsidiaries, etc.

A number of audits in the early 1980s resulted in substantial payment to participants due to the studios underreporting home video revenues. Those who did not audit were eventually barred by the contractual statute of limitations and suffered the loss of substantial participation payments.

In the home video industry's early years, the 20% royalty was reasonable. Home video distributors faced the extremely high costs of organizing a brand-new industry. Marketing expensive hardware with little available software, finding manufacturers to make those funny plastic boxes, packaging, warehousing, supporting retailers, etc., required a large percentage of the wholesale price.

However, as the industry matured, costs began to decrease rapidly. While duplicating, marketing, and distributing a videocassette in 1982 could easily cost $40 per unit, the same cost today is roughly $3. Even so, the industry clings stubbornly to the 20% royalty as its standard.

EXCEPTIONS TO THE 20% ROYALTY RULE

There are exceptions. New guild agreements negotiated in the late 1980s provide that residuals are tied to the "producer's share," in effect the 20% royalty. The fact that these guild agreements effectively cap the residual amount payable for home video, and the fact that the 20% royalty in studio contract language is a *de facto* standard that is non-negotiable for the vast majority of participants, distributors feel better able to grant certain *select talent* and producers (read "star talent") a greater share of the video rental without worrying that this practice will create an expensive precedent.

Royalties of up to 40% of wholesale for those select few are not uncommon. Larger independent producers, those who provide much of their own development and financing and rely on the studios for their distribution system only, have been able to negotiate net video deals, earning a share of gross video revenues after fees and expenses.

Still, deals in excess of the standard 20% royalty remain notable and rare.

Inequities of the 20% Royalty

The inequities of the 20% royalty are further compounded by deductions the net profit participant is charged. In a typical motion-picture industry scenario, all services, including manufacturing and distribution, are provided by the (nearly always captive) home video company, which then reports its 20% royalty. Yet the standard net profit-participation agreement allows the film distributor to charge its own fee against the 20% home video royalty, usually 30% in the domestic market and 40% for foreign.

To understand how that works, lets look at Sharon Seduction's profit statement. *Power Lunch* earned $190 million in domestic wholesale video revenues, and $93 million in foreign:

20% domestic royalty reported	$38,000,000
20% foreign royalty reported	18,600,000
33% combined domestic/foreign distribution fee	(18,678,000)
Total participation after all fees	**$37,922,000**

In this scenario, even though *Power Lunch* earned $283 million in home video revenue, and Sharon Seduction is nominally entitled to a 20% royalty, only $37.922 million or 13.4% of the home video revenue is counted toward her net profit share because the studio effectively takes a distribution fee twice, first through its captive video company, and then on the 20% royalty.

In addition to reductions by distribution fees, the profit participant's share is further reduced at most studios by additional expenses.

Since the guild agreements now call for residuals to be paid on "producer's share" (i.e., the 20% royalty), distributors charge the entire residual amount (which equals approximately 18% of the 20% royalty) as a distribution expense.

Also, the amount charged as dues and assessments at most studios includes a substantial payment to the Motion Picture Association of America for its video anti-piracy work. Even though these expenses are incurred on behalf of the member companies' home video businesses, the costs are allocated to individual pictures, and thereby to the profit participants, on the basis of a film's theatrical distribution.

The upshot is that at some studios, what begins as a supposed pure 20% royalty is reduced by fees and expenses to approximately a 10% to 12% royalty.

There is always a legal, contractual basis for this reduction. Still, the end result is that the participant loses the benefits of between 80% to 90% of a major portion of the motion picture's revenue.

Whether or not this is fair lies in the eye of the beholder. Without dispute, this is one of the most controversial areas of profit participation accounting.

PAY-TV/BASIC CABLE

FADE IN:

INT. OFFICE — DAY

David and Bernie sit at a table covered
with computer-generated reports, examining
documents and making notes on yellow pads.
There is a knock on the door.

>   BERNIE
>   Come in.

There is a fumbling sound.

>   MUFFLED FEMALE VOICE
>   Can someone help me?

David gets up from the table and turns
the handle on the door, which flies open
as a young blonde woman in a red T-shirt
and blue jeans, JENNIFER, carrying a
heavy document box, stumbles through the
doorway, almost colliding with David. He
grabs at the box to steady her, and for a
brief moment they are face to face, gazing
into each other's eyes for the first time.

                    BERNIE
          Oh, good! The pay-television back-
          up. Why don't you bring it over
          here?

Bernie clears a place on the cluttered table
for the box.

                    DAVID
          Let me help you.

                    JENNIFER
          No. It's all right. This is my job.

Neither let go of the box, which is marked
"HBO." Instead, they both guide it to the
place Bernie cleared. Bernie bursts in
between them, enthusiastically opening the
lid, like a child after a prize.

                    BERNIE
          What have we here?

                    DAVID
               (still in a semi-
               dreamlike state)
          I asked for the pay-TV records. I
          hope this is the right stuff.

Bernie looks left and right, and sees what
is happening. He smiles.

                    BERNIE
          It is. At least, it is if the box
          really has the Home Box Office deal
          records inside.

He begins rummaging through.

                    BERNIE
          By the way, David, meet Jennifer.
          Jennifer, David. David is my
          assistant on this audit. Jennifer
          is an intern at the studio — and
          an aspiring producer. You finish
          your master's degree in film at
          USC this year, isn't that right?

Jennifer nods, trying to regain her
composure.

                    JENNIFER
          If you need anything else, just
          ask.

                    DAVID
               (weakly)
          We will.

Jennifer backs out of the door, flashes
a quick smile, and disappears. David
blushes. Bernie rolls his eyes.

                    BERNIE
          Okay, David. So tell me about pay-
          TV.

David returns to earth. But he looks
puzzled.

                    DAVID
          I always think of HBO as cable.

                    BERNIE
Think some more. Take a look out
that way.
          (pointing to the northern-
          most window.)
What do you see?

                    DAVID
Just some satellite dishes on top
of a building. They look just
like the one my uncle has in his
backyard, only bigger.

                    BERNIE
          (laughs)
Not much like your uncle's dish,
either. Those dishes are how the
studio delivers films to HBO/
Cinemax for play on pay-TV. They
also explain why pay-TV isn't
cable, even though it can be found
on cable television. Understand?

David looks puzzled.

                    BERNIE
Okay, so not yet. Let's just say
that in profit participation, pay-
TV has enough impact to be counted
all by itself.

                                   FADE OUT

DOMESTIC PAY-TV

In pure dollars flowing to the profit participant, its not unusual for pay-TV revenues to fall second only to theatrical. This is a key market for motion pictures, and a major industry in its own right.

The vast bulk of pay-TV license revenues flow from Time Warner-owned Home Box Office/Cinemax, Viacom-owned Showtime/The Movie Channel, and independent Starz/Encore. At this writing, every studio has an output deal with one of these three broadcasters, meaning that the entire feature-film output of every major is destined to play for pay on one of the major pay services. This provides a certain stability and predictability in this particular market, with the caveat that the business is ever-changing.

Pay-TV began as a cable-television phenomenon (basic cable will be covered in the next section), but today is delivered into the home by a multitude of technologies. Consumers can pay for premium programming through their local cable-television operator, pay for individual service transmissions downloaded directly from an orbiting satellite using a three-meter backyard dish, or pay for a package of signals beamed into a thirteen-inch mini-dish mounted on the roof. Whatever the delivery mechanism, pay-TV is a firmly established market for exploiting filmed entertainment product.

Pay-TV output agreements are vivid examples of how theatrical play affects a film's earning ability in every other market.

A typical pay-TV output agreement might look something like this:

First, we calculate the base license fee:

Box Office Gross	Base License Fee
< $5,000,000	= 50% of Box Office Gross
$5,000,000 to $9,999,999	= $2,500,000 plus (40% of revenue over $5,000,000)
$10,000,000 to $24,999,999	= $4,500,000 plus (20% of revenue over $10,000,000)
$25,000,000 to $59,999,999	= $7,500,000 plus (10% of revenue over $25,000,000)
$60,000,000 to $99,999,999	= $11,000,000 plus (5% of revenue over $60,000,000)
$100,000,000 to $199,999,999	= $13,000,000 plus (2% of revenue over $100,000,000)
>$200,000,000	= $15,000,000

(In addition, some contracts adjust the base license fee according to the number of subscribers the pay-TV service had added/lost since the output deal was signed.)

So, under this sort of agreement, a film like Revolution/Columbia's renowned bomb *Gigli*, which earned under $6 million, commands a pay-TV license fee in excess of 40% of its theatrical rental earnings. At the same time, Warner's *Harry Potter and the Sorcerer's Stone* would be limited to $15 million for its license, even after its box office climbed stratospherically above the $300 million mark.

In Sharon Seduction's case, *Power Lunch* earned $275 million at the box office. So under the studio's output deal, the pay-TV license was worth $15 million.

There have been some unusual output deals made where the royalty is tied to production cost rather than to film rental. These generally provide a license fee at some fixed percentage of the negative cost, most commonly 50%. However, these are not the norm in the industry and understandably so—$20 million in the can does not necessarily translate into a like amount at the box office. Just ask the producers of *Gigli*.

In general, all pay-TV deals require that any given film play on a minimum number of theater screens for a minimum number of weeks supported by a minimum number of advertising dollars to qualify. The reason for this goes back to the notion that theatrical exhibition is the locomotive that pulls the motion-picture train.

Foreign Pay-TV

The foreign pay-TV markets are much more diverse than those in the United States, though the major players have tremendous influence in the motion picture market. France's Canal Plus is an important European outlet and also has a history of being an aggressive co-producer of Hollywood pictures. British Sky Broadcasting is active in England and parts of Europe; Star Television in Asia.

FREE-TV

In the olden days, free-TV meant broadcast TV. As the manner by which filmed product is delivered into a home television takes on less and less relevance, free-TV is more and more a term attached to advertiser-supported television of any kind, be it distributed by network, syndicated broadcast, or cable.

On a participation statement, domestic free-TV will always be broken out into two separate line items: network television and syndication television. Foreign broadcast-television receipts from all sources are simply attributed to free-TV.

NETWORK TELEVISION

There are essentially two flavors of contracts describing just what constitutes network television revenues. One defines "network" as revenues flowing from any one of the "big three": ABC, CBS, or NBC. The "other" names any revenue derived by any "national network" as fitting the network television definition.

In the olden days, both contracts referred to the same creatures, since only the big three operated as national networks. But the mid-1980s brought the Fox network onto the scene. So now, depending upon which contract the participant signed, any revenue from Fox might appear as either network or syndication television.

The difference can be significant for the profit participant because of the difference between network and syndication distribution fees charged by any studio. The standard network distribution fee is 25% of the license fee paid by the network to the studio. The standard syndication fee is 30% to 40% from a major studio and as high as 50% from an independent. Distributors justify syndication fees being higher than network fees by arguing that distributing to syndication television requires more effort than selling to a single network. As is discussed in greater detail below, syndication often means negotiating many separate licenses with numerous individual television stations scattered about the United States. A network sale, on the other hand, requires only a single contract with a single entity.

Enter the Fox network. A sale to Fox is equivalent to a network sale in terms of ease and simplicity, and under the general rationale, should be subject to the lower network distribution fee. Even so, some contracts limit "network" to the big three, which means the participant is charged the higher syndication fee for Fox revenue even though the distributor worked no harder selling to Fox than it would have selling to ABC, CBS, or NBC.

Films are generally licensed to network television on a one-by-one basis, with each license fee being essentially whatever the market will bear. At this writing, high-profile films with network appeal can command up to 15% of their domestic film rental as a network license fee.

Just how important network revenues are to a film project varies from picture to picture and depends heavily upon marketplace demands. In the early 1980s, network revenues were at their peak. A $10 million license fee wasn't unusual at that time, and theatrical films regularly played to national audiences. Every network had its movie night, be it *ABC Sunday Night at the Movies* or *CBS Night at the Movies*.

Then, in the mid-1980s, the rise of Home Box Office, Showtime, and other pay-TV services that fed audiences theatrical films without commercials almost immediately after their theatrical release prompted the networks to essentially abandon theatrical films in favor of product produced exclusively for network airing. So the situation comedy and hour-long drama became the network staple, and only the biggest event films ever found their way to network.

Today, networks are again licensing hit theatrical films, generally for two showings in a set period of time. The network sale is again becoming an increasingly important source of film revenue.

SYNDICATION TELEVISION

Historically, syndication television was the business of packaging motion pictures for sale to individual television stations, station groups, or advertiser-supported cable services. The syndication window is generally two to three years following theatrical release.

The market has changed drastically with the advent of basic cable channels specializing in the broadcast of feature films.

Stations such as Lifetime and the Turner Movie Channel have replaced local stations as the vehicle for syndication.

FOREIGN FREE-TV

Licensing to offshore advertiser-supported television is accomplished in very much the same way that pictures are sold in domestic syndication. Films are sold as packages of titles, the license fees are allocated among various films in the package, though the formulas used for making the allocations are often even more mysterious than those used domestically.

The creativity of the allocation system becomes most apparent in the foreign free-TV market. For example, Japan has a customs tax on imported theatrical films. Legend has it that it is not at all unusual for a Japanese programmer who purchases a film package to only pick up a few select titles from customs, and leave the rest waiting. The better to avoid paying taxes on films that won't ever be aired anyway. Still, those reels resting quietly in some customs lock-up are earning their license fee allocations, even as their more popular comrades are toiling on some projector in some steamy Tokyo control room. If you are a participant in one of the popular titles, you might find this unfair. If you are a participant in one of the dogs, chances are you will never see a profit participation dime anyway.

Still, somewhere out there, a studio accountant is smiling.

MERCHANDISING, MUSIC, RECORDS, MISCELLANEOUS

Depending on the film, this category can represent zillions of dollars or pennies.

It's beyond dispute that Hollywood motion pictures can create marketing opportunities far more valuable than their direct earning abilities. Merchandise tied to theatrical films represents a multi-billion-dollar industry on its own. Not that this has always been so.

In the early 1970s, a young film director made a small motion picture that proved to be a major smash. The director had a deal for his next film at a second studio, and since a hit film always means that the talent wants to renegotiate its deal, it was no surprise when the production executive's telephone rang.

Only, much to the executive's surprise, the film director wasn't asking for more money. Instead, the director's attorney asked if the studio wouldn't agree to give up all merchandising rights.

In the early 1970s, merchandising rights were considered next to valueless. The studio had no problem giving them up to the young director.

The director's name was George Lucas. His lawyer was Tom Pollock, then a partner with the entertainment powerhouse Pollock, Bloom & Dekom, later president of Universal Pictures theatrical motion pictures division. The film was *Star Wars*.

Today, George Lucas is a very wealthy man.

CHAPTER THREE

THEATRICAL DISTRIBUTION

Theatrical motion-picture distribution requires art, science, and a sprinkling of witchcraft.

Technically speaking, theatrical distribution involves licensing the right to exhibit motion pictures on a rental basis to theaters and creating and disseminating advertising and publicity to support theatrical play. It also requires generating the film prints used in exhibition, and then delivering, storing, inspecting, and repairing those prints during the theatrical run.

From a non-technical standpoint, theatrical distribution involves a complex web of business relationships, market demands, and arcane custom and practice.

LICENSING AGREEMENTS

Theatrical distribution starts with a licensing agreement between distributor and exhibitor. This agreement sets the essential terms for the motion picture's theatrical play.

Distributors negotiate license agreements with exhibitors on a picture-by-picture basis. These agreements contain all the material terms by which the film will be exhibited: They specify what film rental will be paid and how long the film must be shown, along with the maximum time it is available for theatrical play.

As discussed in an earlier chapter, film rentals are usually based on a percentage of the exhibitor's box-office receipts. Occasionally, rentals will be licensed on a flat-fee basis, but rarely during a picture's initial run. A flat fee is more common for second-run theaters (which play films that are past their initial release) or where the distributor is renting select screens (a practice known as "four-walling," which will be described in more depth later).

Exhibition terms, along with availability for theatrical play, vary depending upon a number of factors.

One key factor is how exhibitors perceive the film will perform commercially in relation to other pictures in release at the time, since theater attendance tends to vary according to the popularity of any given picture in release and marketplace competition from other films playing at that same time.

Also important is the time of year that a film is released. The peak U.S. and Canada attendance periods are the summer months, the Christmas holidays, and Easter season. The reason is simple: The core film audience are teenagers and young adults in their early to mid-twenties. When school is out, a teen legion traditionally heads for the movie theaters to check out the latest films. This phenomena is so predictable that distributors always keep a calendar close at hand when plotting their marketing strategies.

The domestic summer season traditionally begins with the Memorial Day weekend in May and ends with the Labor Day weekend in September. The Christmas season begins with the Thanksgiving weekend in November and ends following New Year's Day in January. The Easter holiday season falls in line with spring break for most schools.

Just as the retail industry counts on Christmas spending for the bulk of its revenue, the film industry relies on Summer, Christmas, and Easter season ticket sales for the majority of its income.

In between the major selling seasons is an opportunity to release pictures appealing to older audiences, specialty films that would otherwise be lost in the high-season clutter, or weaker projects that can't stand strong competition. Release timing, in short, is key.

AND "B" TITLES

As important as timing is the quality of the product that a distributor wants to place in the theaters.

Motion pictures are generally broken out into two major categories: the "A" title and the "B" title. "A" titles are generally understood as being films with larger budgets, established stars with strong marquee appeal, and wide theatrical distribution. That combination carries with it a presumption of broad audience appeal, and describes a film at the top of the Hollywood pecking order.

Even so, there are many memorable dogs whose pedigree fit the "A" title definition but failed to attract box-office interest. Michael Cimino-directed *Heaven's Gate* had the big budget and star appeal that made it an "A" picture out of the gate. But that major flop nearly sank United Artists, and many argue that it was a prime reason that UA's then-owner, TransAmerica, sold the studio.

On the other hand, "B" titles are usually defined as feature films with cast or other elements that give them a narrow audience appeal but which also receive wide theatrical distribution. These pictures include those more modestly budgeted films released theatrically on a limited or regional basis. However, just as an "A" title doesn't necessarily mean stellar box-office proceeds, neither does a "B" designation mean less potential. Miramax's *Pulp Fiction* starring John Travolta was a modest-budget production, but wound up grossing in the $100 million range, a pure "A" title performance.

Even so, the "A" and "B" title concept is important in distribution, since before a film hits the theaters, everyone's crystal ball is equally clouded. "A" titles can generally be counted upon to command the best terms and screen locations; "B" titles by definition have less clout in the marketplace.

DISTRIBUTION PATTERNS

Theatrical distribution patterns vary from distributor to distributor and picture to picture. But the common denominator is that the pattern of distribution is dictated by what the distributor believes will result in the highest revenue from the theatrical market.

"Well duh," you say? The problem is, the marketplace is continually evolving. So release patterns are constantly being adapted to fit emerging market conditions.

WIDE RELEASE

In recent years, the wide release has become the dominant means of introducing a major film to the theatergoing public. Generally,

a wide release involves booking the picture to open simultaneously on 1,000 or more screens nationwide following a national
media campaign aimed at boosting consumer awareness about
the particular film. It is no longer unusual for major releases to
open on 4,000 screens during the peak seasons.

Generally, opening day is Friday, which catches the first
weekend-date filmgoers and others who are out on the town at
the end of the work/school week. Friday night, Saturday, and
Sunday will account for as much as 80% of the total tickets sold
in any given week.

Some films follow this same pattern but open on a Wednesday
night. These are generally pictures that the distributor believes will
benefit from strong word of mouth by early viewers. The notion
is that the Wednesday and Thursday night play will increase the
weekend audiences by a substantial margin.

For ninety-nine out of one hundred pictures, opening weekend marks the high point for ticket sales, with each succeeding
weekend showing a percentage decline, until the film finally leaves
the theaters. Sometimes, though, a film unexpectedly catches fire
and builds from its initial release. *My Big Fat Greek Wedding* is
the classic example of that sort of behavior. The picture opened
modestly, gained strength, and then played and played and played.
When a film holds up well, week after week, we say it's got great
"legs." Longevity can be as important to a film's commercial
prospects as a big open.

For major releases in the peak summer and Christmas
season weeks, the present practice for distributors is to target

approximately 3,000-4,000 screens for a wide release. This strategy is based on the solid principle that for 99% of all wide releases, the opening weekend is when the most tickets are sold, so the more seats available, the better the ability to capitalize on market demand.

While the wide release is common, it is by no means the exclusive pattern available to the canny distributor.

Different films demand different handling. Not every picture is a $100 million Brad Pitt vehicle, or would even benefit from the kind of distribution pattern an "A"-grade studio film requires.

PLATFORMING

The opposite of a wide release is the distribution pattern sometimes called "platforming."

This pattern is often used for what are labeled "critic's pictures," i.e., films that the distributor believes will not perform well in middle America without favorable reviews from the critics.

In this situation, the distributor might open the picture only in New York and Los Angeles, receive critical acclaim (and the accompanying word-of-mouth publicity), and then, based upon this acclaim, spread the engagements (probably rather slowly) throughout the country.

In the 1970s, *The Deer Hunter* was successfully released by platforming. The fact that you likely have heard of *The Deer*

Hunter gives testament to this strategy's effectiveness, when properly utilized.

A typical platform release might look like this:

First Three Weeks: First-run exclusive or open only in first-run theaters and only in one such theater to a market area. A city or a defined geographical area may be considered as a market (in some cities, such as Los Angeles, there is more than one market area).

Second Three Weeks: The next group of engagements might also be restricted to first-run theaters, but may include more than one house per market. (If a picture opens in one first-run theater and then moves over to another during its initial engagement, this is called a "move-over.") Depending upon many factors, including how the picture is performing, engagements already booked, and competing product, this second stage of release may be extended beyond three weeks.

Third Three (or Six) Weeks: The distributor may now decide to open the picture in as many theaters as it can book, limited, of course, by how many prints are available. This run (or "wave") is sometimes called the "wide multiple" portion of the platform run.

Fourth Six Weeks: Finally, the distributor may decide to take bookings in the neighborhood theaters and in the smaller towns within each market. This phase of the release pattern may be called the "sub-run."

The Wide-Multiple

In between platforming and the wide release is a hybrid pattern usually referred to as the "wide-multiple."

Suppose the distributor has rights to *Chop Sock 'Em IX*, a ninja-sci-fi sequel to the original low-budget cult classic. What the picture lacks in story and production value it makes up for in dross and tedium, but the posters expose lots of flesh on mostly unclad, but heavily armed, nubile teenage girls, and there's a built-in audience out there.

In a case like this, the distributor will often decide to take its money while it can. That will mean opening directly in a very wide-multiple release, booking 1,500 to 2,500 engagements. The film opens and closes in one weekend, but before word of mouth cuts off the stream of theatergoers, the maximum available revenue is safely in the till.

Even so, just because a picture is opened in such a manner does not mean that the distributor considered it an exploitation picture with stubby little short legs. There might be a variety of reasons for this sort of distribution pattern, and the distributor will generally remain sufficiently flexible so that they may deviate from their plan to open and close quickly if a picture unexpectedly grows legs and outperforms initial expectations.

Special Handling

Another type of distribution that had varying success in the 1970s and early 1980s was called "special handling" or "saturation marketing."

Typically, this strategy involved "four-walling," that is, renting and/or operating theaters in a particular market for a particular picture, and then promoting the film with large media advertising expenditures in that select market area.

A famous salvage of a rather dismal national release was achieved in the early 1970s when *Billy Jack* was re-released in this manner after bombing in its initial run. The result was a commercial showing strong enough that the picture spawned at least one rather-forgettable sequel.

An independent distributor, the now-defunct Sunn Classic, was successful in the 1970s and early 1980s utilizing saturation marketing techniques to release such family-oriented fare as *In Search of Noah's Ark* and *Gentle Ben*. While uncommon today, there's no telling when market conditions will dictate that special handling is again a viable release option, especially for small independents.

Independent distributors sometimes utilize a form of special handling by opening a picture in only a few select markets. This is done for several reasons.

A motion picture might only be opened in a few select markets to limit the print and advertising dollars risked on the initial release. Once the picture proves itself commercially, the distributor is free to invest additional releasing-cost dollars for advertising and prints without having gambled large amounts on a potential bomb.[1]

As release costs have skyrocketed, the pressure to avoid a costly release debacle is at a historical high. One historical victim to that pressure was *Theodore Rex*, a $33.5 million family comedy starring Whoopi Goldberg and distributed by New Line Cinema in 1995.[2]

Word that *Theodore Rex* was bypassing theatrical release after an unsuccessful test-market run cropped up just four days after Whoopi Goldberg hosted the 1996 Oscar ceremonies. "If Goldberg's Oscar night gig celebrated all that was right with Hollywood, her *Theodore Rex* experience epitomized many of the things that can go wrong," wrote the *Los Angeles Times* in reporting the decision to sidestep theaters. The *Times* went on to detail a troubled production, including a $20 million breach-of-contract lawsuit against Goldberg that was settled by the actress agreeing to perform in the picture for a $7 million fee.

New Line reportedly paid $5 million for *Rex*'s domestic distribution rights. Since the average 1995 cost of releasing in the theatrical market exceeded $17.5 million, the financial risk New Line faced by proceeding with a theatrical release far exceeded the cost of acquiring the picture itself.

[1] This is a different distribution scheme than a platform release in that platforming assumes that a limited release will be broadened, while special handling anticipates that wider distribution will only occur if the market demand justifies it.

[2] Elaine Dutka, "'Rex': Extinct on the Big Screen," *Los Angeles Times*, April 4, 1996.

A limited release might also be chosen in order to meet specific requirements contained in contracts for ancillary markets like pay-TV or home video. These contracts often specify not only the required minimum amount of advertising and print monies that must be invested, but also specify how many engagements must be opened. In some cases, the contracts will even specify what markets the picture must be opened in to quality for specific license or royalty payments.

DISTRIBUTOR ORGANIZATIONS

MAJORS, MINI-MAJORS, AND INDEPENDENTS

The companies engaged in the motion picture industry have often been classified as either "majors," "mini-majors," or "independents."

Majors are divisions of the large, vertically integrated entertainment enterprises that include such familiar names as Universal Pictures, Warner Bros., 20th Century Fox, Columbia Pictures, TriStar, Paramount Pictures, and Walt Disney Pictures.

Generally, the majors own their own production studios—including studio lots, production soundstages, and post-production facilities—and have a nationwide and/or worldwide distribution organization. The majors typically release a greater proportion of "A"-level motion pictures—the average cost of producing a studio film, termed the "negative cost" (for the cost of creating the motion picture negative) exceeds $63 million at this writing. The majors provide a continual source of motion pictures to the exhibitors, so they have bargaining leverage commensurate with their status as regular supply sources.

At this writing, here are the major theatrical motion-picture distributors in the United States:

Buena Vista, Touchstone, Hollywood Pictures (Walt Disney)

Columbia Pictures, TriStar Pictures, MGM, UA (Sony)

Paramount Pictures (Viacom)

Universal Pictures (NBC/Universal)

20th Century Fox Film Corporation (News Corp.)

Warner Bros. (Time Warner)

Once, the mini-major was an active category in distribution. Today, such entities are history, though the mini-majors are still mentioned in contemporary motion-picture contracts (in part out of habit, in part as insurance against resurrection of the mighty mini).

"Independents" generally do not own production studios and may or may not provide a continual source of pictures to exhibitors.

During the past five to ten years, the majors have acquired or created independent and specialty film distributors in a massive industry-consolidation wave. Some of the major-owned specialty distributors include:

New Line Cinema (Time Warner)

Focus Features (Universal)

Miramax (Disney)

Searchlight (Fox)

True independents, distributors that provide their own financing and distribute wholly independent of the majors, are a dwindling breed. Even so, the independent spirit and tradition remain strong, and this category, like the South, shall inevitably rise again.[3]

Though not domestic distributors themselves, another category of company bears mention. Independent producers, such as New Regency Films, do not own their own domestic distribution, but instead distribute their films domestically through the majors. Because they have their own financing, they are able to negotiate preferred distribution terms and have better control over their own destinies than producers who depend totally on the studios for capital.

---

[3] The independents still functioning today represent the hardy remnant of what was a thriving and active industry in the late 1980s. During the end of the Reagan era, capital was flowing into the independent film industry in vast amounts, and the foreign presales market was particularly aggressive. Companies such as Cannon Films, New World Pictures, De Laurentiis Entertainment Group, and their kin produced scores of lower-budget productions that they distributed themselves, both domestically and overseas. However, the boom collapsed with the world economy in the early 1990s, and most of the major independents entered bankruptcy, were acquired, or went out of the motion-picture distribution business. The result is a smaller, though arguably healthier, industry today.

The Motion Picture Association of America

Most distributors are joined together in a trade association known as the Motion Picture Association of America (MPAA), formerly headed by the industry's legendary lobbying powerhouse, Jack Valenti, who was replaced in 2004 by former congressman Dan Glickman.

The MPAA is on a constant vigilance for legislation that would be contrary to the best interests of motion picture distribution (e.g., state sales tax on film rentals or FCC financial interest and syndication rules), piracy and illegal use of motion pictures, as well as the rating of motion pictures' content (G, PG, PG-13, R, and NC-17 rating system).

The organization is funded through a dues assessment levied against each member—later we will discuss how that dues assessment is allocated between pictures and how it affects the profit participant.

The current MPAA members are the six major distributors.

Distribution Clout

Substantial investment is required for prints, advertising, and other releasing costs, an average of close to $100 million (including negative cost)[4] for each major studio release as of this writing.

---

[4] The number climbs every year. According to the MPAA, the average negative cost for a major studio film was more than $63 million during 2004, while the average print and advertising expense exceeded $34 million.

Then there is the special distribution expertise required to successfully launch a picture, the systems and procedures required for delivering the physical prints and tracking accounts payable, as well as the incalculable value attached to personal relationships between distributors and exhibitors.

Because exhibitors prefer to deal with distributors who have track records for getting prints and materials to the theater on time and supporting advertising in the media to coincide with the theatrical exhibition, the field is skewed hopelessly in favor of the majors. At least for the time being.

However, occasionally producers will attempt at least an initial release (maybe by four-walling in one or a few theaters in one market) when they cannot obtain a distributor for their pictures or when they cannot come to terms with distributors. This is a high-risk undertaking because producers as a class have little leverage over exhibitors.

DISTRIBUTION FEES

The distribution fee is the film-rental amount retained by the distributor in accordance with the contractual provisions of its agreement with the outside participants. In theory, the fee represents the distributor's fixed-distribution overhead costs. However, how and when distribution fees are charged are often areas of dispute between profit participants and distributors.

The distribution fee is generally expressed in terms of a percentage of revenue by source. The percentage may vary by geographic distribution area as well as by market source. For example:

Theatrical Distribution	Fee
United States and Canada	30%
Foreign	40%
Television Distribution	
U.S. Network	25%
Syndication Sales	30% to 40%
Pay/Cable	30% to 40%
Miscellaneous	
Non-Theatrical Distribution	30%
Home Video	30%
Merchandising	50%

These fees are intended to compensate distributors for their selling efforts and for maintaining their home office, branch offices, worldwide sales organization, the use of funds for release costs, and other expenses. In the case of *Power Lunch*, the collective distribution fees for all sources was $111,000,000, or one-third of the total gross receipts.

Not all motion pictures, however, generate phenomenal distribution results. Which means that the decision to distribute a motion picture is by its nature a high-risk decision. Often, the distributor is unable to recoup even his distribution expenses, much less retain any of the distribution fee. The abbreviated example, below, is much more typical of motion picture distribution results than the accounting that we reviewed earlier for *Power Lunch*:

Total Gross Receipts	$6,000,000
All Distribution Fees	2,000,000
Distribution Expenses	8,000,000
Deficit	**$(4,000,000)**

In the above example, the distributor was unable to recoup its $8 million distribution expense and none of the $2 million distribution fee due. If the distributor had additional investments, such as a non-returnable advance to the producer, those would also be lost.

Based upon publicly available information, here are the "boilerplate" distribution fees of the major distribution companies:

RECEIPTS/REVENUES FROM THEATRICAL & TV[5]

	Domestic	U.K.	Foreign	Flat Sale
Paramount (1)(2)	30%	35%	40%	15%
Warner Bros.	30%	35%	40%	15%
Columbia (3)	30%	35%	40%	15%
20th Century Fox (4)	30%	37.5%	40%	15%
Walt Disney Pictures	30%	35%	40%	15%
Universal Pictures	30%	35%	40%	15%

---

[5] Source: *Buchwald v. Paramount* litigation exhibits.

(1) Paramount and Disney charge a 25% distribution fee on a U.S. television network license fee.

(2) Paramount, Warner Bros., and Disney charge a 35% distribution fee on license fees from U.S. television syndication.

(3) Columbia includes receipts from Canada in the category on which it charges a 35% fee. All other distributors include Canada as a domestic source.

(4) 20th Century Fox charges a 37.5% distribution fee on receipts from the U.K. and from continental Europe.

Distribution fees on royalties or other receipts might vary depending upon how the royalties or other receipts are computed.

The distribution fee may be a *negotiable* factor for an outside third-party participant (such as a financing source) depending upon negotiating strength. The percentage rates are usually standard and bear little resemblance to actual costs. If a producer were to supply the releasing costs (the so-called "rent a distributor" approach), a lower distribution fee can usually be negotiated. Also, depending upon the leverage of the producer/profit participant, a sliding-scale distribution fee might be negotiated.

An example of this:

Theatrical Distribution	U.S. & Canada	Foreign
First $50,000,000	30%	40%
Next $25,000,000	25%	35%
Over $75,000,000	20%	30%

However, is it ever appropriate to have a lower distribution-fee percentage because of the successful performance of the distributor? Or is successful performance always due to a picture's inherent merits, and the distributor is only incidental?

Some producer/profit participants who have the negotiating leverage will opt for a participation share in the gross receipts (which really isn't the gross receipts, as discussed below).

This gross participation might start after a breakeven, say $40,000,000:

Gross Receipts	$100,000,000
Contractual Breakeven	40,000,000
Balance	60,000,000
One-Third of Gross to Participant	**$20,000,000**

Or in some other manner, such as after an advance of $5,000,000:

Gross Receipts	$100,000,000
Gross Participation (@ 20%)	25,000,000
Less Advance	5,000,000
Net to Participant	**$ 20,000,000**

It might involve an accelerated rate, depending upon how certain the distributor is in obtaining receipts at the lower levels. For example:

First $50 million @ 5%	$2,500,000
Next $50 million @ 35%	17,500,000
Total to Participant	**$ 20,000,000**

Some independent distributors may compute their distribution fee in a different manner. They might deduct certain distribution expenses "off the top," that is, before computing their distribution fee. For example:

Gross Receipts	$100,000,000
Off-the-Top Expenses	20,000,000
Balance	80,000,000
Distribution Fee @ 50%	40,000,000
Other Distribution Expenses	20,000,000
Net Proceeds to Participant	**$20,000,000**

The above example works out the same regardless of whether there is a 40% distribution fee on gross receipts or a 50% distribution fee after the deduction of off-the-top expenses. This is not a coincidence. The distributor has the same costs and will want the same compensation regardless of how it computes the distribution fee.

In fact, calculating a distribution fee after off-the-top expenses can result in a larger distribution fee. Off-the-top expenses, as described above, would be contractually defined in the distribution agreement. They probably would include licenses and taxes, collection costs, checking costs, costs of converting foreign monies to U.S. dollars, residuals, and could also include such items as trade dues and assessments and local advertising.

Of course, negotiating a distribution agreement where all distribution expenses come off the top may be possible.

For example:

Gross Receipts	$100,000,000
Distribution Expenses	40,000,000
Balance	60,000,000
Distribution Fee @ 66²/₃%	40,000,000
Net Proceeds to Participant	**$20,000,000**

In sum, although a major distributor's distribution fee may appear relatively high, it may also be well worth it. In general, the major distributor is able to command better license terms, is better positioned to expertly market the picture, and is far more capable of collecting film rentals due from exhibitors than are the smaller independents with less market clout.

HOME VIDEO

The major theatrical distributors all have their own video distributors. Presently, here are the major players:

Warner Home Video (Time Warner)

Paramount Home Video (Viacom)

Fox Video (NewsCorp.)

Buena Vista Home Video (Walt Disney Co.)

Columbia TriStar Home Video (Sony Entertainment)

MCA Home Video (Universal)

Independents remain a force in the home video industry, though as the majors began to insist on home video rights for most pictures they distribute, obtaining product has become an ever-increasing problem for independents. At this writing, at least one independent home video distributor, LIVE Entertainment, is producing its own product to help fill its distribution pipeline.

The independents fill a market niche by distributing a broad range of home entertainment software such as audio CDs, tapes, and video products, along with specialized merchandising services to mass merchandisers such as Target, Kmart, or Wal-Mart. This specialty business is known as "rackjobbing."

A rackjobber will provide its customers with a wide range of merchandising, inventory control, and other services that the merchandisers require in order to manage their retail sales operations. The services often include planning department layouts, designing and installing display fixtures and signs, and working with the merchandiser to determine optimal product mixes by taking into account such factors as customer profile, selling season, and consumer trends. Rackjobbers will even create advertising for their accounts. The goal is to fill a void that the major distributors cannot service.

TELEVISION DISTRIBUTION

The television window typically is broken up into two parts: a network window and a broadcast/cable syndication window. The network window generally follows directly behind home video, while the syndication window typically follows any network availability, and may stretch out over a multi-year period.

Motion picture licensing to commercial television is generally accomplished by an agreement that allows a fixed number of telecasts over a prescribed period of time for a specified license fee.

Typically, United States network licenses extend from one exhibition during a two-year period to four or five exhibitions during a six- or seven-year period and provide for exclusive television exhibition by the network licensee.

Television exhibition license fees vary widely, depending upon the perceived or actual popularity of the picture involved and whether the picture is licensed individually to a national network in prime time or is part of a group of pictures licensed to local stations or cable operators.

In some cases, television syndicators will license pictures on a cash-plus-barter basis. These agreements require a fixed cash license fee, plus a fixed number of commercial minutes that the distributor reserves to sell on its own account. These agreements are usually sold to local television broadcasters or station groups. The distributor's goal is to license or "clear" broadcast outlets to reach a maximum percentage of national television homes. When performed successfully, these "barter networks" act as ad hoc national networks, giving the syndication distributors the opportunity to sell a national advertising vehicle.

Barter networks give rise to "make-goods," a term referring to commercial time sold to an advertiser with a guarantee as to share rating when that guarantee isn't met. When that share isn't met, the barter syndicator must make good with additional advertising time.

For the profit participant, the amount of revenue recognized and when it is reported can be particularly complex where a theatrical picture was licensed for broadcast under the barter method.

Chapter Four

DISTRIBUTION EXPENSES

FADE IN:

INT. OFFICE — DAY

David and Jennifer are foraging among a
head-high stack of document boxes piled
against an entire office wall. At the
table, Bernie keys columns of digits into
his laptop computer.

Jennifer uses one crumbling cardboard box
as a step to reach the very top of the
pile. Suddenly, it gives way, throwing
her completely off-balance. Grabbing for
a handhold, she dislodges a storage box
avalanche and, for one terrifying moment,
tons of paper threaten to crush her
against the cold office floor.

Flying through the air like a college
football tackle, David grabs Jennifer by the
waist and pulls her clear from the collapsing
cardboard column of death. They tumble to the
floor together, and for a precious moment,
lie there catching their breaths together.

Bernie surveys the wreckage with obvious
concern.

                    BERNIE
          Looks like some studio file clerks
          have secure jobs for a few more
          years. Are you both okay?

Jennifer reluctantly pulls herself from
David's arms.

                    JENNIFER
          I'm okay. But look what I've done!

Documents lie loose in waist-high piles,
scattered loose from their broken boxes. It's
a huge, unsorted mess. Jennifer sinks slowly
to the floor.

                    JENNIFER
              (realization taking hold)
          That's it. I'm going to be banned
          from the lot for the rest of my
          life.

She gazes forlornly at the mess. David
brushes himself off as he regains his feet.

                         DAVID
                    (consoling)
               Don't talk like that. I'll help you
               put everything back. No one will
               ever know what happened.

                         JENNIFER
                    (close to tears)
               You're wrong. We'll never be able
               to sort through this mess. There's
               no way to tell what goes where.
               It's hopeless.

Bernie is looking somewhat amused.

                         BERNIE
                    (kindly)
               Actually, I think you've lucked
               out. This is not really as bad as
               it looks.

He reaches down a grabs a sheaf of papers.

                         BERNIE
               These are all distribution
               documents. They were sorted by
               type, so it shouldn't be that hard
               to put them back into some kind of
               order.

                         DAVID
               But they're all jumbled together
               now. And everything looks the same.

                    BERNIE
          Not true. For instance, these are
          ad agency invoices.
                    (he reaches down and
                    grabs some other pages)
          These, on the other hand, are
          residual check stubs. Obviously they
          don't go together. But look . . .
                    (he grabs two other
                    fist-fulls of documents)
          here are some bills from the
          outside publicity company,
          and these are receipts from a
          featurette. Obviously, they came
          from the same box.

David and Jennifer are both looking at
Bernie blankly.

                    JENNIFER
          Obvious to you, maybe.

                    BERNIE
          No. Obvious to anyone who knows how
          a studio exploits a picture. Sure,
          these are all about distribution
          expenses. But if you know the
          business, distribution expenses
          break down into some fairly
          recognizable categories.

                                        FADE OUT

ADVERTISING AND THE DOMESTIC THEATRICAL DEBUT

After artistic quality and popular appeal, the most important factor in a determining a film's ultimate financial success is the theatrical marketing and advertising campaign. An aptly tuned campaign can make a good picture into a blockbuster, or turn a potential bomb into a modest performer.

Since the success of any film is generally determined during its initial domestic theatrical run, a strong, effective advertising campaign can directly affect the terms that the distributor is able to receive in every successive market.

For distributors, a theatrical advertising campaign is a complex creature. Typically, in overseeing a theatrical ad campaign, the distributor will take on such diverse tasks as determining the marketing approach, supervising the creation of advertising material (including pressbooks, trailers, and other promotional material), and arranging for the advertising, publicity, and promotion of the film.

The distributor will also spend huge amounts of dollars on national promotion through television, radio, magazine, newspaper, and trade-journal advertising. Indeed, for 2004, the MPAA reported that the average studio picture cost $34.4 million for prints, advertising, and marketing.

Except for the rare picture with strong enough "legs" to support a lengthy run, the major portion of all print and advertising dollars is spent before even one dollar of film rental is earned.

The Campaign

Needless to say, the details of the theatrical advertising and marketing campaign are of compelling interest to the profit participant. So take comfort in the knowledge that modern motion-picture marketing campaigns are as finely tuned as modern methodology permits.

That includes prerelease market testing. Just as in any modern industry involving products marketed to the masses, the distributors will apply a variety of audience-sampling techniques designed to aid in focusing the marketing and advertising effort before most motion pictures are released.

Advance Screenings

A classic testing technique is the "sneak preview," an advance screening that provides the opportunity for a broad audience reaction before opening day. Just as a disastrous sneak sparked a total makeover of the fictional silent-film-turned-talkie-turned-musical in MGM's classic *Singing in the Rain*, today's advance screenings can still have tremendous impact on how a film is marketed, and even how it will look.

When Universal was in the final weeks of readying the Kevin Costner epic *Waterworld* for its summer 1995 release, director/star Costner used a series of out-of-town sneaks to gauge audience reaction and help fine-tune the nearly $200 million project. Perhaps there was a time when artist/creators felt obliged to trust their own visions over those of test audiences. Today, filmmakers tend to seek out any edge they can get. (The costs of sneak previews will be discussed later in this chapter.)

Short of a full sneak preview open to the general public, distributors will also retain marketing-research consultants to conduct "focus groups," where the nascent picture is shown to a small, demographically hand-picked audience for their opinion. One advantage of the focus group over the sneak preview is that a private focus-group showing tends to eliminate the problem of eager critics reviewing a film before opening weekend.

TRACKING STUDIES

Before, during, and after the picture's initial release, distributors generally conduct ongoing market-tracking studies to measure public awareness and interest.[1] The tracking studies are the distributors' primary tool for deciding how to best use their precious marketing dollars. A film that demonstrates strong promise usually warrants additional spending, as may a picture that needs an awareness boost before opening day. On the other

---

[1] A "tracking study" is a research study that tracks the marketing campaign for a film prior to and following opening day.

hand, where the tracking studies show a film as a likely dead-on-arrival loser, there's an opportunity not to shovel dollars into a looming economic black hole.

COOPERATIVE ADVERTISING

One way that distributors get extra impact from their marketing dollars is through cooperative advertising. Co-op ads are advertisements paid in part by the distributor and in part by the exhibitors.

In the pages that follow, we'll consider whether certain types of marketing activities may be considered cooperative or theater-level advertising. Although the topic is discussed in greater detail later on, the profit participant needs to be aware up front that in some agreements, including some talent personal-service contracts, co-op advertising deductions are included in the off-the-top deductions that are taken before even a gross participant's participation is calculated.

In some contracts, the distributor's distribution fee is computed after the deduction of off-the-top expenses, so the distributor will attempt to limit the number of expenditures considered in this category. However, in the case of a gross participation to an outside third-party participant, the distributor has an incentive to try to maximize the number (and amount) of expenditures included in the off-the-top category. In that case, the amount of co-op advertising expenses may become a big issue for both the distributor and the participating talent.

TRADE ADVERTISING

In addition to the ultimate consumer (the theater patron), advertising must be directed to certain entities in the trade. For the motion picture industry, trade advertising means appearing in one of the two daily Los Angeles-based trade papers, *Daily Variety* or *The Hollywood Reporter*, or taking an ad in weekly *Variety*, which reaches the east coast and Europe.

The film business is a people business first and foremost, so communicating with other players in the creative community has a direct economic value, even if it is not easily measured. For example, when a film is still in the planning stages, trade ads might be aimed at actors, directors, writers, and other talent with the simple goal of making the talent community aware that the producer or studio is actively supporting and pursuing a particular project. The idea is to entice key talent into getting involved with future projects or the actual project being promoted.

This is not to say that there is never an ego angle. For example, producers generally recognize that the more visible they are in the trades, the more seriously they are treated as they shop new projects around Hollywood. Likewise, directors and actors benefit from being publicly connected with their new projects, which improves their prospects of landing another picture. Perception, in a business where illusions are peddled for profit, can be a determining factor for future success.

Still, if talent awareness and ego were the only reasons for taking an advertisement in the trade newspapers, the distributor or financier might better spend the money elsewhere.

A more tangible reason for trade advertising is to make potential distributors aware of a project for which distribution isn't already lined up. These ads might tout the producer for buying movie rights to an important novel, signing up a major star, or commencing principal photography. Even so, since these advertisements may appear as much as a year or so before the release of a motion picture, their benefit on the distribution results is rather speculative.

A third type of trade advertising is directed at the exhibitor. These ads may take the form of a multi-paged, four-color, slick inserts appearing in *Box Office* or *Film Bulletin*, two trade publications that cater to the exhibition crowd, as well as *Variety* and *The Reporter*. These fancy four-color inserts are sometimes drafted to do double duty—it is not unusual for distributors to mail the inserts separately to exhibitors, along with an invitation to bid on the picture.

In addition to the insert, the distributor may send a small promotional item (such as a paperweight, a pen, a calendar, etc.) to the exhibitor, advertising the coming release. Another standard device is the product reel, a five-to-fifteen-minute film of edited scenes from the motion picture, compiled and screened for the exhibitor even before the motion picture is complete.

After a film's opening, trade advertisements trumpeting a picture's box-office receipts are common for successful releases. These ads aren't only directed at theatrical exhibitors as a way to encourage them to treat a picture as a preferred product, they are also aimed at buyers in the secondary markets (video, television), since box-office receipts are a strong indicator of audience demand and ratings potential once the theatrical run comes to a close.

DECIDING WHO PAYS

Whether all of these types of marketing costs are distribution expenses separately deductible on an outside participant's statement computing "net profits" or are really sales costs rightly absorbed by the distributor as part of its distribution fee is a matter of contractual interpretation. It's also an area for potential dispute.

During a participation audit, allocating marketing costs will often arise as a key issue for discussion. Though the contract nominally decides who pays what costs, that same contract generally will permit the studio to charge advertising costs once as a distribution expense, and then add a 10% advertising overhead fee to cover any in-house marketing costs. Most studios will also allocate a portion of the cost for their in-house staffs and charge that portion as part of their general marketing expenses.

Because the studio is also charging a flat overhead fee on top of marketing costs, the area spawns some interesting dialogues as the studio and the participants grapple with what expenses are legitimate charges and which are double-billing—the "overhead-on-overhead" that the court found objectionable in the Buchwald case.

NETWORK TELEVISION

Network television advertising is a major tool for promoting motion pictures during a national release. Even so, network television has both strengths and weaknesses as a marketing tool.

The cost of network television commercials ("spots") may be 25% or 30% less than if those same time buys were made locally in all of the covered markets. However, exhibitors do not share in the cost of network time, as they might share in a local spot through cooperative advertising.

Network commercial time must be secured well in advance of the release date, often as much as a year in advance in order to ensure desirable time slots. If the time is purchased close to the release date, the cost will be at a premium and it is doubtful that the exact, desired slot can be purchased. If the purchased network television time cannot be used, it may be sold to a media buying service at a large discount. Late buys are at a premium and late sales are at a discount.

Network television advertising is expensive. So, since a network television campaign can cost millions of dollars, the television-time purchase may well dictate the motion picture's theatrical release date. This can be a burden, especially if the picture is behind schedule and can't be finished in time to mesh with a pre-paid advertising schedule.

Since the timing of the network campaign dictates when the picture will open, it can also force the distributor to book engagements at less than optimal terms or in less than optimal theaters. If the best screens aren't available when the ads are running, the second best will have to do. Likewise, if an exhibitor can use the leverage of an impending high-profile network campaign as a means of extracting more favorable license terms from the distributor, it will. For that matter, if any given picture is not ready for release at the time scheduled for its network television campaign, and the distributor doesn't want any of the options specified above, it may release another picture instead of the one it originally intended to release.

Network availability doesn't just affect release patterns, it can have a direct impact on the quality of the film as well. For example, the timing pressures imposed by a pending network campaign might dictate that a picture be released before it is satisfactorily completed.[2] When this happens, occasionally a better version of the picture might be released later in a second theatrical wave or used for television.

Still, despite its disadvantages, network advertising is almost always used for major theatrical releases. And what distributors want to tell their producers that their pictures are not major theatrical releases?

---

[2] This is also becoming more and more common during such peak seasons as summer, when the studios typically schedule their strongest titles in hopes of reaping huge grosses. In fact, the problem has been so pronounced that film editors have become vocal with their complaints that by being forced into rushed editing schedules, the quality of their films is declining.

Cooperative Advertising

Though this term has evolved into meaning almost all local advertising, cooperative advertising historically meant that the exhibitor and the distributor shared (cooperated) in the cost of the advertising.

This sharing, if it still exists, has transmogrified into everything from participation by the exhibitor in the cost of all media; participation by the exhibitor in only selected media (distributor paying 100% of the costs of non-selected media); and even to the point where the only contribution made by the exhibitor is the cost of electricity and the plastic letters on the theater marquee.

The methods of sharing these costs vary by distributor, vary by market (city), and may even vary by release from the same distributor. For example, in a first-run situation in New York City, the distributor, by custom, normally pays 100% of all advertising costs. In other markets, and depending on the distributor (and the picture), the exhibitor may agree to a set amount as a contribution toward the cost of the local advertising campaign; may pay all of the newspaper cost, while the distributor pays the cost of all other media; may participate in 50% or some other percentage of the costs; may share up to a maximum specified amount; etc.

Also, the sharing arrangements (and which costs are to be included) may be an area open to negotiations after the engagement is concluded.

The co-op media placement ("buy") may be done by the exhibitor, by a local or national advertising agency, or directly by the distributor. The advantage of exhibitor placement, primarily in newspaper advertising, is that local exhibitors can leverage their annual advertising volume (called "lineage use") into an ad rate that is much lower than that available to the distributor or even to an ad agency.

ADVERTISING AGENCIES

Advertising agencies often procure co-op ads. Their expertise generally lies in knowing the advertising time availabilities and how to purchase (or sell) them.

The agencies traditionally bill at a 15% commission rate. However, agencies aren't paid 15% of their media invoices. Rather, the 15% commission is actually a 17.65% rate:

Invoice Net Amount	$ 85.00
Agency Commission	15.00
Invoice Gross Amount	**$100.00**

($15.00 divided by $85.00 equals 17.65%)

So, if an agency is retained to provide a television commercial and the cost to produce that commercial is, say $200,000, the cost to the distributor will be $235,300 (and not $230,000). For a major media buy, the difference is worth noting.

The commission rate is intended to compensate the full-service agency, including the indirect costs of creative efforts, media and campaign planning, local representation, publicity planting, market research, etc. As the motion picture distributor may utilize an agency only as a media buyer, a rebate of some portion of the commission may be negotiated. If the agreement is for a 50% rebate of the commission, that amount would be 8.825% (50% x 17.65%) of the net media costs.

The amount of this rebate can become quite significant on a motion picture that is heavily advertised on the networks. The outside participant should be concerned that the distributor has properly reported this rebate as a reduction in the advertising. The timing for reporting the rebate versus reporting the incurrence of the costs is a potential problem area in determining the breakeven point for the outside participant.

Some exhibitors utilize an "in-house" advertising agency. They might require that all media purchasing be done through their agency and might not rebate any of the commission to the distributor. They are able to do this because of the relative power they may have in a particular market area. Although this practice might be considered "competition in restraint of trade" or questionable under some other antitrust legislation, if the distributor wishes to book a picture in a particular market area, it will do what it believes necessary to make the deal.

FOUR-WALL ADVERTISING

At one time, four-walling was a fairly common way of distributing films, especially for independents. The practice has largely died out, but the method remains viable. Because the four-wall cycle might rise again, it is worth examining how advertising costs are reconciled. The four-wall type of arrangement is quite common outside of the United States.

The term "four wall" refers to a procedure by which the distributor becomes responsible for the theater for a specified period of time. Depending on the various contractual terms, this could mean that the distributor rents the theater and directly employs all personnel working there (the classical definition). Four-wall has also come to mean that the distributor guarantees to pay the exhibitor a negotiated overhead amount to cover rent, utilities, personnel, other operating expenses, and may allow the exhibitor a profit (i.e., guaranteeing the house nut). If the box-office receipts are not adequate to cover the agreed-upon amount, the distributor pays the difference. Another permutation of this type of arrangement (which might not be considered strictly as a four-wall engagement) is a 100% film rental deal. Under this arrangement, the exhibitor is entitled to first box-office receipts up to the negotiated amount, and any excess goes to the distributor. In the 100% film rental deal, if the box-office receipts are less than the negotiated amount, the exhibitor bears the deficit. (The type of exhibition deal negotiated is a matter of need and relative power at the time of the negotiation.)

There are some legal (antitrust) ramifications relative to a distributor acting as the exhibitor of a motion picture. When a distributor is unable to book an engagement in a suitable theater, in a given market, and at acceptable terms, it may attempt to negotiate a four-wall deal. This may be necessary due to a network television-time buy, which will be telecast in that particular market area.

All four-wall advertising (local advertising for four-wall engagements) might be classified by the distributor as cooperative advertising. Additionally, any deficit between the box-office receipts and the house nut may also be classified as cooperative advertising. If not specifically spelled out in the participation contracts or if there is a difference between the terminology in the participation contracts and the exhibition contracts, a dispute may arise.

Universal's Net Profits Exhibit "A" defines four-wall engagements as follows:

> [Four-wall] means engagements for the exhibition of the Photoplay in theaters hired and/or operated by Universal for the respective engagements. Income received by Universal from each four-wall engagement in any country shall be included as Accountable Gross from the respective country, but only if and to the extent that such income exceeds the expenses of hiring and/or operating the theater for that engagement (such as theater rental and salaries of theater help). All other expenses of four-wall engagements (such as advertising expenses) shall be deducted under the appropriate provisions of Paragraph A6. If the expenses of hiring and/or operating the theater for any such four-wall engagement exceed such income from that engagement, the excess shall be deducted under Paragraph A6, as a distribution expense.

Interesting! If the 100% of the advertising is charged as a distribution expense (instead of only a co-op share as in non-four-wall engagements), then shouldn't the participant share in the net results from the concessions (assuming the distributor does)? How many distributors' accountants would interpret this to mean that the participant should share in the popcorn and candy receipts?

Sneak-Preview Advertising

There are at least three distinct types of sneak previews.

Director's Sneak

The first is a preview of the "director's cut," that initial version of the film edited to the director's initial vision. The producer and the distributor must agree to this preview (i.e., bearing the cost thereof) in accordance with the DGA agreement. The number may be increased to two or more previews depending upon the negotiations of the personal-service contracts with the director and others.

The "director's cut" preview is usually not held in a major metropolitan area where it might be accessible to critics or where public word-of-mouth would have any substantial effect when the picture is eventually released. As a result of the audience reaction to this preview, the director may shorten/lengthen certain parts of the film, change the ending, or otherwise alter the picture. Take the case of *Fatal Attraction*.

The film is about a very-married New York lawyer (Michael Douglas) who is seduced by a blonde associate (Glenn Close). While the Michael Douglas character has a one-night stand in mind, Glenn Close, as the eerily unbalanced other woman, begins a terror campaign aimed at destroying Douglas's family.

Originally, the film ended with Glenn Close vanquished, but free to fight another day. When the picture ran in previews, the filmmakers discovered that the audiences *hated* the idea that Close could essentially get away with near murder. So, they killed her—the Close character, that is. The film's ending changed. The picture opened as a smash hit, and remains one of the hot films of the 1980s.

Local advertising is employed to help secure full audiences for previews. The cost of this advertising may be classified as a production cost (subject to contractual overhead rates) rather than a distribution expense.

TRADE SNEAK

The second type of preview is called the "trade sneak." Although the advertising, theater rental, and all other associated costs may be classified as advertising and publicity costs (i.e., distribution expenses), the primary function of this type of preview is for sales purposes. Therefore, it might be effectively argued that the expense of this type of preview should be absorbed by the percentage distribution fee and these charges should not be separately deducted as distribution expenses in the motion picture accounting.

In a trade sneak, the exhibitors in the area are invited to view the picture with a live audience. (A trade screening without an audience is generally considered as a sales expense covered by the distribution fee, although some distributors may not agree with this.) Following—or as a result of—this preview, the exhibitors are invited to bid on the picture. The trade sneak usually takes place several months before the release of the movie.

WORD-OF-MOUTH SNEAK

The third distinct type of sneak preview, which is called the "word-of-mouth sneak," generally occurs only two or three weeks prior to the release of the motion picture. In these sneaks, the public is invited to experience a new picture at a special time and place before its official opening debut. The purpose of this preview is to generate enthusiasm and word-of-mouth publicity about the coming release. All costs associated with this type of sneak are properly classified as advertising/publicity expenses. As these sneaks usually take place shortly before the picture opens, some distributors consider the costs as part of the pre-opening advertising campaign and, therefore, properly classify them as cooperative advertising.

ADVANCE ADVERTISING

Another type of consumer advertising (versus trade advertising) is the advance teaser campaign. In these campaigns, the title of the motion picture is rarely announced. Advertisements try to build interest in one of the elements, generally the starring player.

Although this advance advertising may be local, it is seldom classified as cooperative or theater-level advertising because no engagement may have been booked at the time and, therefore, the advertisement does not include the name of the theater.

THEATER ADVERTISING

Probably the best advertising dollars spent (with the most returns at the box office) are in advertising at the local theaters directly before a film opens. In addition to the marquee and theater paper (posters, standees, window cards, still photographs, etc.), theater advertising includes the ubiquitous theatrical trailer.

The first trailer (previews of coming attractions) to be created for an advertising campaign may be the teaser trailer. Classically, this is the short (90 seconds) film that is shown as much as six months to a year before the release of the movie being advertised. The teaser trailer may contain no film footage from the motion picture; it may have live-action footage different from the foot-age of the theatrical motion picture; or it might consist only of a title card, some artwork, music, and narration.

The regular theatrical trailer is usually longer than the teaser trailer and averages 2½ to 3 minutes. Usually, scenes from the motion picture have been edited into this advertising film, which, consistent with all of the advertising materials, are selected to emphasize the marketing approach (some factor of the movie that is likely to have the greatest consumer appeal). If a trailer advertises a motion picture showing at another theater, it is termed a "cross-plug" trailer.

Both Walt Disney Pictures and Paramount Pictures in their standard Net Profit Exhibit "A" boilerplate contracts define Negative Cost of production to include the trailer:

> The cost of production (or direct cost) is the aggregate of all costs, charges, claims, and expenses paid or incurred in connection with the development, production, and delivery of the Picture and its trailers, including payments required to be made at a later date following production of the Picture, determined in the customary manner. . . .

Both also define trailers as an Advertising and Publicity Cost under Distribution Costs. This may be a leftover from the days (prior to the 1970s) when National Screen Corporation would prepare trailers during the production of the motion picture and would then distribute the trailers (for a fee paid for by the exhibitor) to theaters.

Surely neither Walt Disney Pictures nor Paramount Pictures would charge an outside, third-party participant for the cost of a trailer in two different categories. However, they might be tempted to charge the larger contractual overhead (production cost versus advertising) if this provision is not negotiated prior to the execution of the agreement.

Unique to the motion picture industry was the practice of selling advertising materials to exhibitors. This practice would equate to a manufacturer or wholesaler selling point-of-sale advertising materials to a retail store. Although this practice no longer predominates in the United States film industry, similar practices are employed in some foreign countries.

CREATING THE PRINT CAMPAIGN

The first artwork created for the advertising of the motion picture is usually in connection with the trade announcements. This artwork may be generated from reading the script or novel, reading a synopsis of the plot, or even less. It seldom becomes the key artwork for advertising the motion picture.

The initial launching of a motion picture is extremely important to its commercial success. The investment in the production cost (usually millions of dollars) is by this time sunk, and the initial launching can help to determine if that investment will be recouped and whether a profit will be made. There is also a distribution theory that if the movie is not properly launched and then not properly supported by advertising, it will never reach its full commercial potential (maximum potential box-office receipts).

The distribution or sales portion of the marketing strategy was discussed earlier under Distribution Pattern. The advertising portion of the marketing strategy fits hand in glove with the distribution portion. Too often, these functions are separated geographically or philosophically in the distributor organization.

The marketing strategy for a motion picture may be based upon the cast (such as a big-named star, e.g., Mel Gibson, Arnold Schwarzenegger, or Tom Cruise), the plot (horror, drama, comedy, etc.), the geographical location, or some other facet of the movie that is anticipated to create wide public interest. One possible approach to establishing the marketing strategy:

- Determine, through market surveys and other research tools, what aspects of the motion picture have the greatest potential for the widest consumer appeal.

- Develop key artwork (album covers, covers for books and novels, movie posters, graphics for newspaper and magazine advertisements, etc.) in accordance with the previously determined market strategy.

- Develop the advertising campaign (media buy) and the publicity and promotional campaigns in a manner that is complimentary to the marketing strategy.

- Determine the appropriate distribution pattern and book the picture accordingly.

Many people (including many with veto power) are involved in establishing the marketing strategy and approving the artwork. In addition to the distributor's advertising and sales staffs, the producer and the director may be involved, the major actor may have a say, a marketing consultant may be retained, the studio's production personnel may take an active role, the advertising agency may be utilized, and the chief executive of the distributor organization (including the chairman of the board of the conglomerate holding company) may make the final decision.

Then, if an impasse arises, the most powerful of all studio personnel will have the final say. (We are referring, of course, to the studio secretary.)

PUBLICITY AND PROMOTION

Publicity is fundamentally different from advertising, and it can have as great or greater an effect on public awareness about any given project. If advertising is defined as paid promotion in any given media, then publicity is the art of coaxing the media into promoting for free.

Publicity runs a long gamut, from trade-press articles to television talk-show appearances by one or more of a picture's creative talent. Publicity includes the critic's review, and though the publicist in charge will have little or no influence regarding whether that review will be favorable, the publicist does have considerable influence as to whether a critic will review a particular movie at all. Publicity includes a cover picture on a national magazine (*Time* and *Newsweek* are particularly prized). Background stories about a film published in the entertainment sections of the local newspapers are also standard publicist fare. Indeed, we are all familiar with the end product of motion-picture publicity campaigns, often to the extent that we as consumers don't automatically recognize that when the *Los Angeles Times* prints a story in its "Calendar" section about a director's latest creative challenge, that story exists as part of a comprehensive marketing and promotion plan for a distributor or a particular project.

So, those familiar guest appearances, articles, and photo layouts are not happenstance by any means at all. Rather, the credit goes to concentrated efforts by publicists striving to raise public awareness about their employers and clients.

PRODUCTION PUBLICITY

In some cases, the publicity campaign starts even before the actual production of the motion picture.

The unit publicist—a publicist attached to and responsible for a particular film—is the individual whose livelihood depends upon an ability to make the public aware of the motion picture production.

The unit publicist is responsible for periodic news releases, designed to keep the media informed about the motion picture's progress during pre-production and filming. The unit publicist will often invite key movie press to the shooting location and arrange interviews with the talent. Other functions include obtaining and writing biographies on the performers, director, or producer for use during promotional activities; supervising the efforts of a still photographer shooting photographs during production; and acting as a coordinator and liaison between the producer's organization (the production company) and the distributor's advertising and publicity personnel.

Historically, all costs of the unit publicist have been included in the production cost of the motion picture, and are subject to the contractual overhead charge. However, if the publicist continues working on the movie after the completion of photography, some question generally arises as to when these same costs become distribution expenses and are no longer classified as part of the negative cost.

PERSONAL APPEARANCE TOURS

One time-honored means of hyping motion pictures is to send the starring performer on a multi-city tour. There, in connection with local publicity efforts (see Field Promotion), the objective is to obtain the maximum media exposure.

A new twist on this standard method is the cyberspace personal appearance. Services such as America Online regularly host online chat sessions with performers and filmmakers as a way of promoting interest in a project.

However the talent appears, the hope is that the media will help stoke the fans into a flaming heat that can only be quenched by sitting in a theater seat.

FIELD PROMOTION

Independent agencies or employees of the distributor are located in certain major cities throughout the United States. The function of these personnel, known as fieldmen, is local publicity and promotion of the distributor's release. This might include planting stories with the local press, arranging displays in local department stores to publicize a picture, arranging promotional contests and giveaways on local radio stations, etc.

Generally, the salaries of advertising and publicity personnel are not separately chargeable (or allocated) to the distribution results of a theatrical motion picture. However, the salaries paid to fieldmen usually are.

The following contractual provision is excerpted from Universal Pictures' Net Profits - Exhibit "A" at Paragraph A6:

> Universal shall be entitled to deduct and retain for its own account, from the Accountable Gross remaining after the continuing deduction of its distribution fees, the aggregate of all sums paid or advanced and all costs and charges incurred by Universal, directly and

indirectly, in connection with the distribution, exhibition, and exploitation of the Photoplay, which are not included in cost of production including any such sums, costs, and charges for or in connection with any of the following:

. . . Advertising, promoting, exploiting, and publicizing the Photoplay in any way, including the following: . . . (iv) Field exploitation, including salaries of employees and allowed living costs and traveling expenses, fees, and charges, whether paid to Universal employees or other persons. . . . (vii) Traveling and living expenses (but not salaries) of Universal's publicity, advertising, and exploitation executives, but only for trips directly attributable to or occasioned by the Photoplay.

In its Net Proceeds - Exhibit "A," Paragraph 5, Columbia Pictures reserves the right to charge all salaries of advertising and publicity personnel to the distribution cost of the picture:

Columbia's distribution expenses shall include all costs, charges, and expenses incurred by Columbia, or a subdistributor accounting to Columbia in respect of the subdistributor's receipts as set forth in Paragraph 2 A (ii) hereof, in connection with the distribution, exhibition, advertising, exploitation, and turning to account of the Picture, . . . including without limitation, all costs, charges, and expenses incurred for or in connection with any of the following:

. . . (B) Advertising, promotion, exploiting, and publicizing the Picture in any way, including without

limitation . . . which Columbia or any subdistributor
pays or is charged with: . . . salaries, living costs, and
traveling expenses of regular employees of Columbia
where such employees are assigned to render services
in connection with the advertising of the Picture,
appropriately allocated to the Picture; . . .

With such an all-inclusive provision, it's reasonable to wonder
just who and what *isn't* charged to a picture.

Another dispute usually arises with respect to a premiere of
a theatrical motion picture. While there is little question as to
the classification of traveling and living expenses of talent and
field advertising personnel, the propriety of charging the picture
with the traveling and living costs of the following personnel
becomes increasingly disputable:

- Advertising and Publicity Executives

- Sales Executives

- Production Personnel (e.g., Production Manager or
  Associate Producer)

- Corporate Executives

(Of course, there should be no dispute as to propriety with
respect to studio secretaries, studio accountants, and attorneys—they are never invited.)

If possible, premiere charges should be clarified during the
deal-memo and profits-definition negotiating phase. Otherwise,

expect any disputable charges will be uncovered during an audit and result in a claim or dispute.

FEATURETTES

Another potentially significant publicity expense is featurette production.

A featurette is a film about the making of the motion picture (the "behind the scenes" story), and usually runs 10 to 20 minutes in length.

The featurette is generally delivered to television stations, usually with no fee attached, though in the past, some featurettes commanded enough interest to warrant a license fee. In turn, television broadcasters, including pay-cable operators and TV networks, generally use the featurette as a time-filler, when regular programming ends between the half-hour periods.

These same featurettes may be used in some foreign countries as shorts between feature showings at the theater.

Any revenue generated by a featurette should, of course, be offset against the cost in the accountings. Due to accounting systems, this may be difficult for the distributor's accountants to do and is even more difficult for the participant's auditors to locate.

OVERHEAD

Most distribution companies charge 10% of the total advertising as a contractual overhead amount. The pertinent provision in the Definitions of Net Profits, Adjusted Gross Receipts and Breakeven - Exhibit "A" of 20th Century Fox Film Corporation as stated in Paragraph VII.D.(g)(ii):

> "Advertising Overhead": An amount equal to 10% of the aggregate of all costs deductible under the preceding Subparagraph (g)(i) to cover salaries and indirect operating costs of distributor's advertising and publicity personnel.

Note that 20th Century Fox does allow for the deduction of "salaries, fees, and living and travel and business expenses of publicists, press representatives, and field and exploitation men. . . ."

Some of the other distribution agreements (in their boilerplate definitions) allow salaries and indirect operating costs of advertising and publicity personnel (or at least, do not disallow them). It may also cover the distributor's cost of monies invested in the releasing costs. Accordingly, during negotiations it is fair to inquire as to what the overhead charge is supposed to cover.

If a producer/financier is furnishing the monies for releasing costs, they may then appropriately request that the advertising overhead charge be eliminated or significantly reduced.

Another consideration during the negotiations might be to request a "cap" or to limit to a maximum the amount of contractual overhead allocable to advertising. In the case of a commercial success, the amount of overhead charged could easily exceed the annual budget of the distributor's advertising department.

CONCLUSION

The cost of advertising and publicity is substantial and may well exceed the production cost of the motion picture. This cost will continue to increase during the foreseeable future.

The precise benefit (dollar of advertising versus box-office receipts) cannot be accurately measured. No amount of advertising can guarantee a box-office success. However, millions of dollars may be lost if a motion picture is not adequately supported by advertising and publicity during its initial launch. So, in that regard, advertising and publicity are indispensable parts of releasing a successful picture.

Chapter Five

OTHER DISTRIBUTION EXPENSES

RELEASE PRINTS

Even though the industry's technical wizards tinker constantly with high-quality electronic cameras and recording systems, to date, no other format is as widely accepted for creating theatrical motion pictures as 35mm film. The fact that motion picture film technology is now more than 100 years old, yet still endures, is quiet testament to the eloquence of this expressive medium.

Of course, motion picture film technology has evolved since the days of hand-cranked cameras and megaphones. From a prospectus by Showscan Film Corporation, a company dedicated to improving the state of the art in motion picture film:

Since Thomas Edison designed the 35mm film format in 1890, 35mm film has been the accepted standard format for the photography and theatrical exhibition of motion pictures.

The original silent motion pictures were usually filmed and shown at a frame rate of 16 frames per second (fps). However, opening and closing the shutter 16 times per second created flicker on the screen. In order to avoid flicker, each frame was shown three times before the next frame was shown, resulting in 48 flashes being projected per second. When sound was added to motion pictures in the late 1920s, a faster frame rate was needed so that the soundtrack on the film could move fast enough past the sound head to produce acceptable sound fidelity.

The standard that was adopted was 24fps, with each frame being shown twice, also resulting in 48 flashes being projected per second. This standard of projecting 35mm film at 24fps remains the standard today.

As theater screen sizes increased, the graininess of the film became more noticeable. In the 1950s, some films were photographed on 65mm film and projected at 24fps on 70mm film in order to increase clarity. In addition, new film projection techniques, including Vista Vision (two 35mm frames projected horizontally as a single frame), Cinerama (three separate projectors using 35mm film), and Todd-AO (70mm film photographed and projected at 30fps), were tried.

In order to reduce film production costs, 65mm filming was largely discontinued in the 1960s. Accordingly, at present, most films exhibited in 70mm are photographed using 35mm film and then enlarged to 70mm film."[1]

---

[1] Showscan Film Corporation, Preliminary Prospectus, April 17, 1987, pp. 16-17.

Though emerging technologies promise wireless motion-picture delivery to theaters of the future, at this point in time, a major distribution expense remains both the cost of creating enough release prints for projection on each and every one of the cinema screens on which the film is being shown across the country and around the world, along with the attendant shipping and handling costs.

When a large number of prints are called for, it is not now usual for them to be made directly from the original picture negative, because of possible damage during the repeated use on high-speed printing machines. Bulk-release printing will therefore be carried out from a duplicate negative, often known as a production dupe, which can be replaced if necessary.

Such duplicate negatives can now be made as color reversal intermediates (CRI) at a single step directly from the original without appreciable loss of image quality and can be printed to incorporate the finally approved scene-to-scene grading of the answer print. Where a very large number of identical copies are called for, second duplicates may be made so that multiple prints can be produced rapidly.

The use of duplicate negatives or CRIs is, of course, also necessary when release prints are required with a different format of image or a different gauge of film from the original. For change of gauge, a corresponding soundtrack negative will be re-recorded from the original magnetic master.

. . . Following inspection, release prints may require final make-up assembly before dispatch; this can include the addition of distribution trademarks and censor certificate titles and individual reels may be joined into larger rolls for projection convenience. At this stage individual prints are given their copy number identification for the distributor's records before dispatch.[2]

A feature motion picture is usually approximately two hours in length. A typical 35mm release print would be approximately 11,000 feet in length (90 feet per minute). 16mm release prints are used for institutions (i.e., non-theatrical) and for a few theaters. The cost per foot is a little less than the 35mm release print, but less than half as much film is needed.

A 70mm release print (sometimes used in selected theaters) costs substantially more than a 35mm release print. Each different gauge will require the use of duplicate negatives or CRIs, and a corresponding soundtrack negative will be re-recorded from the original master. In addition to the print costs, the cost of reels, inspection, cases, rewinding, replacements, and sometimes freight may be included as Release Print Costs in the motion picture accounting.

Foreign release prints may be struck in the United States or in a foreign country, depending on the lab capabilities and working arrangements. The laws in some countries require that the release prints be dubbed and reproduced within that country. In that situation, the film elements—including picture, music, sound effects, but no dialogue—will be shipped to the foreign country for processing there. The costs of these elements, the freight, and the dubbing costs may all be classified as Release Print Costs.

[2] L. Bernard Happel, *Your Film & the Lab—2nd Ed.*, 1983, Focal Press.

A potential area for dispute between the distributor and the outside participant is whether a charge is properly classified as a production cost (subject to the contractual overhead charge) or a distribution expense. Generally, costs incurred prior to the approved answer print might be considered production costs, and any costs incurred subsequently might be classified as distribution expenses. The approved answer print is the first producer-approved, color-corrected print where the image and the sound are married. The answer print will be discussed further under Production Costs later in this book.

As with all generalities or rules of thumb (especially in the motion picture industry), the concept that costs incurred prior to the answer print are negative costs and costs incurred after the answer print are distribution expenses has a number of flaws.

For instance, what if the picture had more than one approved answer print? The best resolution of the classification problem is to understand the film laboratory process and the usage of the various negative and positive film materials. (Hint: It wouldn't hurt industry attorneys and accountants, as well as distributor sales personnel, to spend some time at the film laboratory.)

As in media advertising with an agency, many film labs allow discounts and rebates to the distributor. The distributor should reflect these as a reduction of the release print costs (not income subject to a distribution fee) in the motion picture accounting. Sometimes, creative souls in the distributor's accounting department will attempt to reserve the entire rebate for the studio alone, rationalizing that the rebate is due solely to the distributor's annual distribution volume. Under this rationale, the picture is not entitled to share in the rebate. However, students of profit participation know that this rationale is misguided, and will treat it accordingly following a participations audit. Sometimes, certain rebates are earned that are applicable to charges incurred during production, but not ascertainable until some time after the production is completed. In these cases, the studio/distributor may not want to open up the books again if the production cost has been finalized for tax, financial, insurance, or other purposes.

The outside participant is not only entitled to the credit, but to an adjustment for the contractual overhead charged on the gross price and included in the production cost. The distributor will not ordinarily object to such an audit claim, but may not automatically report the adjustment (particularly as to the overhead reversal), unless claimed by the outside participant.

A number of video costs might also be properly included under the Release Print category. These include the cost of the transfer from film to videotape and the one-inch duplicates (known as dubs) prepared for television broadcast. Some television stations may broadcast using a 16mm print or a ¾-inch videotape, but the one-inch gauge is the usual material for television broadcast in the United States.

The format used in the United States for ½-inch home video is known as NTSC (formally the National Television Systems Committee standard, but often referred to as "Never Twice the Same Color"). NTSC has 525 scan lines, of which 480 are active for defining the image. PAL (Phase Alternating Line) is the format used in Europe as well as many other areas. PAL has 625 lines to define the image. SECAM (Sequential Couleur Avec Memorie) is a third format used in some Asian countries.

TAXES

DOMESTIC TAXES

Which taxes, if any, are chargeable to a motion picture and reflected in the accounting to an outside participant is a matter of contractual provision as well as custom. Income taxes, for example, are seldom chargeable, but in some situations sales taxes or other taxes may be chargeable.

Is it proper to include sales or other taxes as receipts, compute a distribution fee on them, and then deduct them as a distribution expense? In its Definitions of Net Profits, Adjusted Gross Receipts & Breakeven - Exhibit "A" at Paragraph VII.B.6., 20th Century Fox Film Corporation excludes collected taxes:

> In no event shall the following be included in Gross receipts:
>
> . . .
>
> 6. . . . any amounts collected by Distributor or Subdistributor or licensee of the Picture as taxes or for payment as taxes, such as admission, sales, and value-added taxes.

However, remittance taxes[3] are usually includable as receipts, distribution fees computed thereon, and then allowable as deductions in the participation accounting. They are usually considered as off-the-top expenses and deducted from gross receipts (along with other off-the-top expenses) in computing the participation of a gross participant.

The logic of this accounting treatment is that a remittance tax (versus a sales tax) is a cost of collecting the money, even though there is a school that believes the distribution fee is supposed to cover collections. Even so, both contractual provision and custom allow the deduction of remittance taxes in computing the gross receipts in which a gross participant shares and in computing percentage residuals for distribution in supplemental markets. On the other hand, no such deduction is allowed in computing the gross receipts on which a distribution fee is computed.

Please note:

NOWHERE IS IT WRITTEN THAT CONTRACTUAL PROVISIONS NEED BE FAIR OR LOGICAL!!!

This is especially the case in the motion picture industry.

Nor is there any rule that accounting for allocating tax expenses need be consistent from distributor to distributor. At MGM, for example, the business-affairs attorneys decided to add an Exhibit "B" to define the distribution expenses deductible under its Exhibit "A" definition.

---

[3] *Remittance taxes* are taxes on money remitted to the United States from a foreign country. These taxes are generally required to be paid under various tax treaties between the U.S. and other nations.

Paragraph 11 of the MGM Exhibit "B" defines deductible taxes as follows:

> The amount of all taxes and fees, however denominated, imposed upon the negative, duplicate negatives, prints, sound records, disks, or other physical property of the photoplay, including but not limited to personal property taxes, if any, assessed upon the photoplay, or any part thereof, after the completion of production of the photoplay; but personal property taxes, if any, assessed upon the photoplay prior to the delivery thereof to the Distributor, in whatever state of completion the same may then be, shall be deemed to be part of the negative cost of the photoplay. Also, the amount of all taxes and fees however denominated, imposed upon, or measured by the gross film rentals derived from the photoplay, including taxes on sales, turnover, gross rentals, percentages of gross rentals, or any part thereof, including any cost of contesting the same. Also, the amount of all taxes and fees, however denominated, upon the conversion of the gross film rentals into United States funds and the amount of all other taxes and fees imposed upon the Producer and/or Distributor or any of its subsidiaries or affiliates relating to or on account of the photoplay or the exercise of any rights under the agreement to which this Exhibit is attached. Nothing herein contained shall be deemed to permit the Distributor, its subsidiaries, or affiliates to recoup any part of its net income, corporate franchise, excess profits, or other similar corporate taxes imposed upon the Distributor, its subsidiaries, and affiliates, as corporate entities, as distinguished from taxes (denominated "in lieu of income taxes" or otherwise denominated) imposed upon the

Distributor, its subsidiaries, and affiliates in respect of the gross film rentals derived from the distribution of the photoplay. In no event shall the recoupable amount of any tax imposed upon the Distributor, its subsidiaries, and affiliates in respect of the gross film rentals or any portion thereof, however denominated, be decreased (nor the gross film rentals increased) because of the manner in which such taxes are elected to be treated by the Distributor, its subsidiaries, and affiliates, in filing net income, corporate franchise excess profits, or similar tax returns. Notwithstanding anything to the contrary contained in this Paragraph 11 or elsewhere in this agreement, participant shall have no right to inspect or copy any tax return of Distributor or any of its subsidiaries and affiliates to produce any such tax return or any information contained therein.

Paramount Pictures Inc. is a little more brief in its Net Profits:

Exhibit "A," Paragraph IV.M.:

Taxes and governmental fees of any nature and however characterized including costs of contesting, interest, and penalties thereon (other than PPC or subdistributor corporate income taxes), imposed directly or indirectly on the Picture or any part thereof (including without limitation the Employer's share of payroll taxes with respect to deferred or contingent compensation) or on the Gross Receipts or the license, distribution or exhibition of Picture, or collection, conversion, or remittance of monies connected therewith.

FOREIGN TAXES

A major distributor will always have a number of motion pictures playing in foreign territories, while at the same time maintaining other offshore businesses as meet its strategic business needs. That means that foreign receipts for any given picture are generally commingled and not separately identifiable. This creates a problem for the profit participant.

The proper accounting method for reporting remittance or withholding taxes would be to apply the statutory rate. However, reasonableness would preclude the use of the full statutory rate against 100% of the film rental earned in a particular country. For example:

Country: Japan	
Tax Rate:	10%
Film Rental	¥10,000,000
Tax at Statutory Rate	¥1,000,000

The calculation should exclude monies that were not actually remitted. For example:

Film Rental	¥10,000,000
Advertising Costs	(¥3,000,000)
Other Amounts Retained in Japan (Prints, Fees, etc.)	(¥2,000,000)

Amount Remitted or	
Which Could Be Remitted	¥5,000,000
Tax @ 10%	¥500,000
Effective Tax Rate	**5%**

In reviewing these charges, participants must take the "what is reasonable" approach. They might be able to require government receipts or returns as proof; however, even if these did not include funds remitted from other motion pictures or other businesses of the distributor, the outside participant would have to master a number of languages and governmental forms to understand the supporting documentation.

GUILD FEES AND RESIDUALS

RESIDUALS ARE A DISTRIBUTION EXPENSE

Another distribution expense on the participations statement are residuals.

Residuals are monies that are paid to actors, writers, directors, musicians, or to craftspeople through the International Alliance of Theatrical Stage Employees (IATSE) for theatrical motion-picture product released on television or in various supplemental markets like home video or pay-TV.

Residuals are considered a distribution expense because they are only triggered if the product is distributed beyond its initial theatrical release. In other words, if a picture never makes it out of the theaters into television or home video, there will never be any residuals paid.

For the purposes of this book, we will only deal with residuals as they apply to theatrical motion pictures as specified by United States guild and union agreements. Made-for-television films, along with pay-TV and home video productions, trigger different formulas and fall outside the scope of this book. Foreign guilds and unions also have different requirements. Be advised: The following is not an exhaustive study of what can be an extremely complex area. For the final word on what residuals apply to which product, you will always need to consult the controlling guild or union agreement. This is also true when determining definitions of "receipts" on which your formulae are determined.

A Brief History of Residuals

Prior to 1960, there was no such thing as residuals. But as network television came into its own, the talent guilds and unions began negotiating for ways to share in a new and important market.

Generally speaking, only films produced after January 30, 1960, are subject to residual payments. The amount of residuals due on any given project is determined by the operative collective-bargaining agreements in effect when the product was created. So, in the earliest days, only free-TV receipts triggered residual payments, which in turn were calculated according to the applicable Screen Actors Guild (SAG), Writers Guild of America (WGA), Directors Guild of America (DGA), etc., collective-bargaining agreements.

SCREEN ACTORS GUILD

Prior to January 30, 1960, SAG members were not entitled to any residuals on theatrical motion pictures. That changed for films produced between January 31, 1960, and January 31, 1966, when the operative SAG agreement provided residual payments for free-TV only. Under the agreement, free-TV is considered to include not only network, but also basic cable, domestic syndication, and foreign syndication. The allocation to talent was based on units, which in turn were determined by the number of days the player performed in the picture, and paid as a percentage of receipts.

The formula was renegotiated for films produced between February 1, 1966, and July 22, 1980. Residuals were no longer calculated as a percentage of receipts, but were instead subject to a formula referred to as the "Base Method." The important change was that under this new method, it became possible for the producer/distributor to be obliged to pay more in residuals than the total dollars taken in as receipts. Another important change for product produced on or after July 1, 1979, was that residuals were now also calculated on supplemental market receipts (in pay and home video).

From July 22, 1980, through October 5, 1980, SAG went on strike, so no product requiring residual payments was created.

On October 6, 1980, yet another formula was adopted. The Base Method was replaced by a calculation based on a percentage of receipts. Residuals were calculated at 3.6% of distributor's receipts (a percentage including pension, health, and welfare payments), with the allocation due actors based on a per-unit value including both time worked and salary earned.

On July 1, 1984, the formula was renegotiated again, with free- and pay-TV triggering a 3.6% residual, allocated to talent by units, and home video delivering a residual equal to 4.5% of the first $1 million of "Employer's Receipts," and 5.4% thereafter.

DIRECTORS GUILD OF AMERICA

Directors Guild of America residuals are, thankfully, much easier to fathom than Screen Actors Guild formulas.

No DGA residuals are paid on product produced prior to May 1, 1960. From May 1, 1960, through June 30, 1971, residuals are paid on free-TV receipts only. Residuals are calculated as a percentage of the distributor's receipts (1.2%) and allocated 50% to the director, and 50% to the DGA Pension Plan.

For July 1, 1971, through June 30, 1984, the formula stayed the same. Residuals are still calculated as a percentage of the distributors gross receipts, but include supplemental market receipts—i.e., pay-TV or home video—with free-TV. Supplemental market residuals are allocated 50% to the director, 33.33% to the DGA Pension Plan, 16.67% to the Unit Production Manager (39% of the 16.67%), First Assistant Director (37% of the 16.67%), and Second Assistant Director (24% of the 16.67%). Where a picture has more than one Unit Production Manager or First or Second Assistant Director, the Guild determines the allocations payable to each.

From July 1, 1984, through the present, free- and pay-TV residuals remain the same. However, for home video releases, the percentage has changed to 1.5% of the first $1 million of Employer's Gross, and 1.8% thereafter. The allocations are 66.67% to the director, 20% to the pension fund, and 13.33% to the UPM (39% of 13.33%), 1st AD (37% of 13.33%), and 2nd AD (24% of 13.33%).

WRITERS GUILD OF AMERICA

Writers Guild residuals mirror the DGA formulae, with the only differences being the effective dates and allocations.

AMERICAN FEDERATION OF MUSICIANS

Residuals are also paid on behalf of participating musicians in any given theatrical picture sold into various free and supplemental television markets. Unlike SAG, DGA, or WGA, these residual payments are made to the Administrator of the Special Payments Fund at the American Federation of Musicians (AFM), who in turn divvies up the funds among qualifying musicians.

The residual rate beginning January 31, 1960, through the present has been 1% of various gross receipt definitions. Until June 30, 1971, the residual only applied to free-TV, since then it has attached to pay-TV and home video as well.

INTERNATIONAL ALLIANCE OF THEATRICAL STAGE EMPLOYEES

Residual payments to the International Alliance of Theatrical Stage Employees (IATSE) go directly to various pension and health plans administered by the union.

Contributions are calculated as a percentage of receipts, with the percentage set at 5.4% of the distributors gross receipts. No residuals are due for product produced prior to January 31, 1960. Free-TV only triggers residuals for February 1, 1960, through June 30, 1971, product.

Films produced between July 1, 1971, and July 31, 1985, require a residual for free-TV, pay-TV, and home video. From August 31, 1985, to the present, free- and pay-TV trigger the 5.4% residual, while home video requires a 6.75% residual on the first $1 million of employers receipts and 8.10% thereafter.

USING RESIDUALS TO NEGOTIATE

Residuals are a significant expense component on the profit participations statement. So it's helpful to understand when they are triggered and who is being paid.

They also provide a useful benchmark while negotiating a profit participation deal. The guilds' agreed percentage of receipts payable as residuals provide base numbers that negotiators representing other non-guild talents, such as producers, utilize in arguing for more meaningful participation in the upside.

TRADE ASSOCIATION FEES AND OTHER ALLOCATED EXPENSES

Some distribution expenses are allocated to the picture rather than charged directly. It is good to pay attention to such expenses.

Included in this category are annual dues paid by the distributor to the MPAA (Motion Picture Association of America). Generally, this assessment is charged based on theatrical performance to each picture released during the year. The dues assessment includes the cost of industry-wide task forces, such as lobbying for stronger copyright and anti-piracy protection overseas.

The MPAA members are the major studios. Because those members are assessed dues based on their grosses from theatrical, television, and home video distribution, allocation amounts charged to each picture become an important issue.

The authors are aware of at least one instance where the assessments that could be charged to the producers of one picture were capped at a maximum amount. When that film wound up a hit of historic proportions, the studio was unable to charge its full assessment to the project. Somehow, the amount that was attributable to that one film, but not charged to it, was allocated among the remaining pictures in the studio's release slate, none of which had caps on their own allocations. The lesson: It pays to pay attention to MPAA dues assessments.

Additional issues are raised as well. For example, some MPAA assessments are for home video anti-piracy protection. So, where a distributor does not have the videocassette distribution rights, profit participants may forcefully require that these assessments are not charged to their picture. By the same token, a theatrical motion picture should not bear the portion of the distributor's MPAA assessments allocable to first-run television programming.

BAD DEBTS

One of the functions covered by the distribution fee is (or should be) the collection of film rental.

Regardless of the accounting method used ("when collected" or "when billed"), a bad debt due to the uncollectability of film rental should not be reported as a distribution expense. Instead, the film rental previously reported should be reversed, as well as the amount of the distribution fee computed thereon.

	Wrong Way	Right Way
Film Rental	$100,000	$100,000
Bad Debt		50,000
Balance		50,000
Distribution Fee @ 30%	30,000	15,000
Balance	70,000	35,000
Bad Debt	50,000	
Remainder	**$20,000**	**$35,000**

Of course, once again the initial participation accounting as recorded by the distributor will be performed in accord with that distributor's custom, as amended by specific contractual terms.

The lesson is to make sure that bad debts are correctly accounted for—the preferred method is to spell out the right computation method in the initial participation agreement.

OTHER DISTRIBUTION EXPENSES

Additional distribution expenses may be chargeable to a motion picture. Some of these might include costs of censorship,[4] duties, checking and theater auditing, special titles, legal expenses and settlements, etc.

Whether these are properly chargeable and properly classified is a matter of custom as amended by contractual provisions and subject to the interpretation of the distributor's accountants.

---

[4] For example, in Malaysia, a distributor must pay a government fee before the official censors will view a film to determine acceptability for play in that country.

CHAPTER SIX

THE PRODUCTION PROCESS

```
FADE IN:

INT. STUDIO OFFICE — DAY

Bernie, David, and Jennifer are working.
Bernie scowls at an open document box
while David and Jennifer paw one-at-a-time
through the cartons lining an entire wall,
searching.

                  BERNIE
             (looking up)
          Find anything yet?
```

                    JENNIFER
          Not yet.

                    DAVID
          Me neither.

Bernie scratches his head and looks about the
room.

                    BERNIE
          They have to be here somewhere.
          Production records don't just
          disappear.

Jennifer slumps against a wall and rubs her
eyes.

                    JENNIFER
          I'm not even sure I'd know them if
          I saw them.
                (she laughs ruefully)
          Some producer I'm going to be. I
          can't even recognize receipts from
          shooting the picture.

                    DAVID
                (hopefully)
          It's not you, Jennifer. They just
          aren't here.
                (looking at Bernie)
          We've been through everything
          twice. There isn't a single scrap
          of . . .

A loud a knock at the door. Bernie walks
over to open it.

                    BERNIE
          Why don't you both take a break.
          Maybe some of the boxes got left
          down in . . .

Bernie turns the handle and the door flies
open. He jumps back, but is nearly run over
by Sharon Seduction as she pushes her way
into the room. Following her are a train of
young men, each pushing a loaded handcart.

                    SHARON
          Let's see. How about, over there.

She points to an empty spot on the floor. A
box mountain quickly rises on the site.

Sharon is dressed casually in white
painter's pants and a striped blouse.
Even without makeup she is strikingly
beautiful. As is her nature, she is also
unapologetically direct.

                    SHARON
          I'm here to help fight for truth
          and justice. I'm also tired of
          being jerked around.
               (She looks intently
               at Bernie)
          You must be Mr. Payne.

Bernie smiles weakly. He is surprised.

                    BERNIE
        Ms., Ms., Seduction. Welcome. I'm
        sorry I'm being so rude. It's just,
        I don't think I've ever had the
        client appear while I was rummaging
        through the paperwork.

Sharon slumps sideways into a chair,
grinning.

                    SHARON
        You've never had me for a client
        before. When it's important to me,
        I like to be there.

The last handcart is unloaded and Sharon
waves as her box-bearers leave the room.

                    SHARON
        Thanks for the help, guys!
                (she turns back to
                Bernie, grinning)
        Guess what I brought you?

                    DAVID
                (peering into the
                top box)
        It's the production records.

Jennifer and David begin organizing the
pile.

                    BERNIE
                (sheepishly)
        I guess I don't understand?

SHARON
          (cheerfully)
What's to understand? I produced
Power Lunch. My company kept all
the records, the better to audit
with.

She winks. She speaks sincerely.

SHARON
I can't tell you how important
this is to me. I've fought my
whole life to star in a big
hit, and I'm not letting anyone
take what's mine from me. They
tell me you're the best in the
business. I'm counting on you.

JENNIFER
Even looking at this stuff, I'm
not sure what it is.

BERNIE
          (Walking over and grabbing
          the top box)
This is the paper trail for the
stuff dreams are made of. You
want to be a producer, Jennifer.
It's not enough to be creative
and have contacts. Business
smarts count, too.

                              FADE OUT

THE PRODUCTION

Motion picture production is a complex, expensive process. Major motion picture production is all of that and then some.

Film production, after all, is a project enterprise. While any given picture can involve hundreds of people and millions if not tens of millions of dollars, no two films are created in precisely the same way.

Even so, a few common denominators apply to most if not all films. To understand how movies are made, it's useful to examine the production as both a process and a cash-eating colossus. Let's start with how things generally work:

THE LITERARY PROPERTY

The theatrical motion-picture development process typically begins with a literary property—a treatment, screenplay, stageplay, or book. The work might be acquired by a production company, or the production company might have it created especially for a specific project.

Once a writer is engaged to write or rewrite a screenplay, a director or individual producer might be brought on board to supervise the writer and prepare a preliminary budget and production schedule.

On the other hand, when a project is being developed by an established talent, the process is somewhat tailored to that individual. Stars such as Tom Cruise have the clout to short-circuit the standard development process and have a film approved on the strength of their interest alone.

Pre-Production

After financing is in place, and usually, but not always, after a final screenplay is approved, the project enters the pre-production phase, where the picture is actively prepared for filming.

Pre-production ideally takes from two to six months, with the caveat that every picture is an individual project, and every project is unique. During the pre-production phase, the production company will hire a production manager and key production personnel, such as the director of photography, special effects supervisor, and other production department heads.

During this period, the principal cast is signed and committed, locations are secured, and budgets and shooting schedules are finalized. On the business side, insurance is put in place, as is a completion bond, if one is required. A start date for principal photography is set, and everyone on the production team begins working under the gun.

Principal Photography

Principal photography is the project phase when actual filming takes place. On the typical studio picture, principal photography generally takes from six to sixteen weeks, either on location, on a soundstage, or both. Principal photography is incredibly expensive, costing tens of thousands of dollars each hour. So when a picture goes over schedule during this phase, it can have a significant impact on the profit participant later on.

POST-PRODUCTION

Post-production is the final creative phase. Post-production generally lasts for four to eight months, during which time the motion picture film is edited into a final product. This is also the time when the music is scored and recorded, dialogue is fixed in place, sound effects added, special effects polished up, and everything is integrated into the emerging motion picture. Preliminary and final cuts are made, the film is screened for audiences—just the production team at first, and then perhaps the test audiences. Finally, the picture opens to popular acclaim, yawns, or somewhere in the middle.

NEGATIVE COST

Though profit participants generally focus their attentions on distribution (because that is when the money rolls in, if ever), production activities and attendant costs are very much a part of the total profit equation.

In Sharon Seduction's case, overall production expenses are lumped into the Negative Cost section of her participation statement. The items included in Negative Cost are Production Cost, Overhead, Interest and Deferments, and Gross Participations. Each item is followed by a large number, so they are all worth understanding.

20th Century Fox defines Negative Cost in its Definitions of Net Profits, Adjusted Gross Receipts & Breakeven - Exhibit "A" in Paragraph VII.E.:

> The sum of "Direct Charges" and "Fox Administrative Overhead Charge":
>
> 1. "Direct Charges": The aggregate of all costs, charges, and expenses, paid, incurred, or accrued in connection with the acquisition of all underlying literary and musical rights with respect to the Picture (including costs of copyright and title searches, clearances and registration, royalty and license fees) and in connection with the preparation, production, completion, and delivery of the completed Picture, including the costs of materials, equipment, physical properties, personnel, and services utilized in connection with the Picture, both above-the-line and below-the-line (including charges established pursuant to the 20th Century Fox Facilities Price Schedule for facilities, equipment, and personnel of the 20h Century Fox Facilities Division furnished and utilized in connection with the Picture, a percentage of all direct salaries established by Fox to cover employer fringe benefits, and costs of insurance). Fox may elect to self-insure any items of risk in connection with the preparation, production, completion, and delivery of the Picture and charge as a Direct Charge an amount equal to the insurance premium Fox would otherwise have paid for such

insurance. Fox shall, in its sole discretion, determine whether or not to obtain or maintain any insurance or to self-insure any item of risk. The amount of losses recovered from insurance proceeds shall be used to reduce Negative Cost.

2. "Fox Administrative Overhead Charges": An amount equal to fifteen percent (15%) of Direct Charges irrespective of where the Picture is produced anywhere in the world.

Just as in Sharon's case, both Walt Disney Pictures and Paramount Pictures include gross participations in the negative cost.

For example, Paramount Pictures Company Net Profit Definition - Exhibit "A" Paragraphs V.A.(2) and V.C.(1):

(2) Participations in Gross Receipts shall be deemed included in cost of production regardless of whether obligation is fixed or dependent upon Gross Receipts provided that the participations in Gross Receipts shall be included in cost of production only to extent PPC obligation to pay said participation accrues before any net profits pursuant hereto have been derived.

The upshot is, gross participations are subject to an overhead charge, a circumstance that was raised as being unfair in the Buchwald case. The rejoinder, of course, is that overhead may be charged because the contract says it may.

PRODUCTION COSTS

PRE-PRODUCTION COSTS

Each year, millions upon millions of ideas come to Hollywood seeking stardom. And each year, thousands upon thousands of ideas are pitched by writers and their agents, producers and their agents, directors and their agents, and agents back to their clients, in an endless stream of hustle and entrepreneurial inertia.

Each year, hundreds upon hundreds of ideas are optioned, acted upon, put on the front burner, or otherwise touted as verging on emerging. And each year, each of the major distributors will release somewhere between ten and forty theatrical motion pictures each.

The point being, the attrition rate for ideas in Hollywood is *colosso stupendous!* To say the least.

ABANDONED IDEAS

Motion picture rights for literary materials such as novels, magazine articles, or even two-page treatments outlining the plot and characters may be acquired or optioned for varying sums of money. However, obtaining production financing, including studio financing, at the idea stage is a difficult undertaking. Needless to say, a high percentage of project ideas are never made into movies.

If a studio project is abandoned, the costs are written off to the studio's overhead. If an abandoned project is financed outside the studio, it will be written off as a loss.[1] Generally, it is inappropriate to charge or allocate the loss from abandoned development deals to other motion pictures for the purposes of accounting to profit participants. However, if a producer has a multi-picture deal with a studio, allocation of these losses to the producer's pictures that *are* made may be appropriate. In this type of a situation, the other outside participants (e.g., the director, talent, writers, etc.) must be concerned that their net profits statements do not include the cost of the producer's abandoned projects and contractual overhead.

Usually, the development phase of a motion picture takes several years, and all kinds of costs may be accumulated as story costs (see The Available Charge Number).

THE AVAILABLE CHARGE NUMBER

Motion-picture cost accounting is a job-order cost procedure, much like that used by a specialty manufacturer or the accounting system used by a service business. Time and materials are "charged against" a job number, which is known in studio parlance as a "charge number."

---

[1] It happens that a financing entity may still own certain developed material, such as a screenplay, even though it does not own the motion picture rights to the underlying literary material. Such scripts are sometimes called *sterile* screenplays, and they have little value without the underlying rights.

The laborer, clerk, painter, editor, or cameraman must charge their time against a charge number if they want a paycheck. Costs not allocated to a motion picture are closely scrutinized and questioned by studio management.

As a result, most time and material charges are made against a picture, regardless of the purpose for which that time and material was used. It is amazing what can be accomplished at a studio by someone armed with an available charge number that the computer won't cough back, acting as though they have the authority (and this *is* a business where acting talents are prized).

Caution: *This available charge number may be the producer's motion picture!* Meaning that, sometimes, just because a charge is allocated to a picture doesn't mean that the dollars were spent on that project at all.

Unless the producers want to bear their share of stray costs that come against their production due to the "available charge-number route," they or their representative will review all charges on a daily or weekly basis. Any questions or objections should be raised immediately and to the right level. This may be the production accountant, the transportation captain, the studio's accounting department, or the studio head.

The objective is to get the charged amount reversed as quickly and as quietly as possible. The producer has the most power during the production cycle and prior to delivery of the finished negative. A post-release audit of the negative cost is superfluous if the producer has performed this function adequately. Audit claims raised a year or two after a questionable cost was incurred and after the motion picture was released may not get the attention or the results that a timely inquiry, conducted without "making waves," can achieve.

One of the authors was retained by the Aldrich Company (director Robert Aldrich and producer Bill Aldrich) to perform this function on a motion picture it was producing at the "old" MGM Studio. Each week, the cost run was compared to the daily call-sheets, the pages of script that were shot during the period, and the lists of props, equipment, and costumes used. Questionable charges were quietly taken up with the studio accounting department.

As a result of this process, *several hundred thousand dollars* in erroneous charges were reversed from the Aldrich picture and charged to the proper picture. If an audit had been performed several years later, it is doubtful that a number of these errors would have been detected.

Facility Charges

Studios will often insist or advise or, at a minimum, strongly hint that filmmakers use production facilities owned by the studio. These facilities can include the studio lot or backlot, special effects companies, or even production services companies.

These production enterprises, which are nominally set up as independent businesses, even though they are wholly owned by the studio, are in the business of renting space and equipment and providing services, generally in accordance with a facilities price schedule. The transactions are designed to function as if they were conducted at an "arm's length" from the parent studio.

Even so, "synergies" are at work where the wholly parent-owned subsidiary does work on a picture being produced and distributed by its parent. For example, an automobile might be charged to a production at a published daily rate (and, hopefully, it was used on that production), which may not only include a rental amount, it might also include insurance, maintenance, fuel, and a factor for profit. This expense is then charged against the picture as part of the negative cost, and is subject to another 15% overhead charge by the studio. This is a good thing—if you are a studio.

For some reason, participants often object to the rates charged by studio-owned facilities as being excessive. A studio-owned production facility, like any facilities business such as a hotel or even a theater, is only profitable if it has a high rate of usage and adequate rates.

Due to location shooting and the large number of productions done in foreign countries, studio-owned facilities businesses usually do not make a lot of profit. An adequate return on invested capital is not too much for the studio owner to seek. Perhaps if studio owners were more open with outside participants, with respect to the financial requirements for operating a studio, there would be a lot less objection to facility rates.

It would not be inappropriate for producers to know exactly what they are getting for the facility charge, something that is often left vague. For example, does the facility rental fee include electricity and air conditioning or are those extra (and at what rate)? The producer has a right to know. Likewise, if the daily charge for an automobile includes fuel, fuel costs should be absorbed by the studio and not charged as a separate item against the picture cost, a practice akin to billing a cost twice.

Studio-owned facilities are often pricey and using them may well be mandatory. Even so, from a purely contractual standpoint, there should be no objection because use of the studio-owned facility at the published rate was agreed to up front.

Payroll Tax and Fringes

Both production and distribution salaries charged to a picture are accompanied by an add-on for supplemental labor costs. This "fringe" amount is intended to cover the employer's share of payroll taxes; health, pension, and welfare costs; workers' compensation insurance; holiday and vacation pay. However, it might also include a profit for the studio, something for which the profit participant should keep an eye out.

In fact, with fringe rates in the 25% to 45% range, depending upon the union and the union jurisdiction (New York fringes are at the high end of the scale), the studios are known to turn fringes into a profit center by always calculating at the highest rate, even if the actual amount paid is less.

The first thing producers should understand is exactly what costs are included in the supplemental-labor cost charge. If this is supposed to cover workers' compensation, then a separate charge for workers' comp insurance would be improper. If it covers holidays, then holiday pay should not be charged to the picture, but should come from the reserve provided by the supplemental labor cost charge.

How much of this can be negotiated up front is questionable. Certainly, if there are a number of highly paid below-the-line personnel (e.g., director of photography, editor, production manager, etc.), it may be appropriate to request a lower rate or a maximum on the amount of supplemental-labor costs charged against these salaries if the components of the supplemental-labor cost have limits (e.g. employer's share of payroll taxes). If the production is to be performed in states or countries with lower payroll taxes or insurance rates, a request for a reduced rate might also be appropriate. However, the supplemental payroll cost or fringe-benefit rate is somewhat sacred and downward negotiation will be difficult.

When the auditors for outside participants in productions done at the studio where Sharon made her deal object to the high supplemental-labor cost rates, the standard reply is, "That is company policy!" This answer, which is received for a number of auditor inquiries, may reasonably be interpreted as meaning that the facts do not support the accounting.

COMPLETION GUARANTEES

Like everything else in the motion picture business, production financing is a risky enterprise. It becomes even riskier if there is no way to ensure that a film will be completed. It's one thing to finance a bomb, where at least the delivery of a finished picture will trigger various contractual payments. It's another thing to foreclose on an unfinished film and have nothing more to show for a multi-million-dollar note than a few dog-eared screenplays and several thousand feet of unedited color stock.

Hence the niche filled by the completion guarantor.

The completion guarantor is usually involved with the production at a very early stage—during pre-production. Since the guarantor will ultimately be responsible for providing funds if a film can't be completed, it will attempt to scrutinize the project as closely as possible, since an ideal world from the guarantor's point of view is one where no film ever gets into trouble and no dollar of premium is ever spent in a rescue.

In evaluating a project, the guarantor will review the script, the shooting schedule, and the budget in detail. Then the guarantor will meet with the producer, the director, the unit production manager, the production accountant, and sometimes the art director and other key production personnel whose views and explanations are appropriate in determining the feasibility of a particular project.

If the review proves favorable, the guarantor may provide a *letter of intent* confirming that it is prepared to write a *guarantee of completion*, subject to certain stated conditions. These conditions include that sufficient financing is available, that the artistic and technical personnel are available as required for the making of the movie, that certain insurance is in place, that location agreements are satisfactory, etc.

The letter of intent will also list certain budgetary items that are considered outside the purview of the guarantor, including publicity, music, legal costs, and finance charges.

In the guarantor's perfect world, the fee for a completion guarantee is 6% of the approved budget, less the contingency (of no less than 10%) and the budgetary items considered outside the purview of the guarantor, and the guarantor's fee itself. However, in the real world, the fee will vary with market conditions, including competition among guarantors, whether or not the production is purchasing production insurance from an affiliate of the guarantor, etc. In recent years, guarantees have been written for as little as 2% of the budget, while the 4%, 5%, and 6% range appears the current standard measure. In addition, the guarantor's fee is generally subject to as much as a 50% reduction depending upon the claims, or lack of claims, made against the completion guarantee.

When the terms of the letter of intent are accepted by the production company and the financiers, the guarantor will review all legal documents relating to the acquisition of the basic story material, the screenplay, and the music to insure that the production company has acquired sufficient rights in order to allow it to deliver the completed movie to the distributors in accordance with the terms of the approved distribution agreements. The guarantor will want to review all agreements for the services of talent and the producer.

The guarantor is not only concerned that the compensation amounts agree with the budgeted amounts, but is also concerned about stop dates vis-à-vis the shooting schedule and the various editing rights given to the director that might prevent timely delivery of the motion picture. The guarantor will also want to review studio, location, and all other agreements.

The guarantee of completion is issued once the guarantor is satisfied that all key documents are in order and a security agreement between the guarantor and production company is executed. This latter agreement contains various warranties on the part of the production company, such as that it has sufficient rights to make the film and that it will do so in accordance with its contractual commitments. The document also gives the guarantor the right to daily progress reports of shooting and weekly cost statements (including forecasts and expenditures incurred) and the right to be signatory on the production bank accounts (a right that is sometimes implemented on request of the financiers).

In addition, the agreement allows the guarantor to require explanations and demand meetings with personnel involved in the production of the movie and, at their sole discretion, to take over the production of the movie in order to ensure that it is delivered in accordance with the guarantee. This final step is not taken lightly and is seldom required.

During production, the guarantor will monitor the progress and costs very closely, both to insure that everything takes place as originally discussed and that the filming proceeds in accordance with the original shooting schedule. The guarantor may be in daily contact with the production company by telephone or, if warranted, may have a representative on location. They may make periodic visits to the location if a representative is not assigned there.

In the event that the guarantor has to advance monies to cover the movie's cost of production, the guarantor is in first position to recoup after all budget items have been recouped. Deferments not in the budget will be paid after the guarantor has recouped any monies advanced.

Overhead or Administrative Charges

Most profit participation definitions from the major studios carry a production overhead charge of 15% of the direct cost.

Although these rates may or may not be negotiable, the profit participant should have the right to know what this charge is supposed to cover and what "overhead type" charges will be classified as direct production costs and, themselves, be subject to an add-on for overhead.

For example, does contractual overhead include:

- The studio's production staff, including scheduling, budgeting, security, maintenance, etc.?

- The salaries and expenses of the studio executives?

- The salaries and expenses of the studio's accounting, data processing, legal, and other administrative departments?

- Parking space for cast and crew?

- Dressing and rehearsal facilities?

- Office rental and equipment for production staff?

- Rental of soundstages (plus electrical, air conditioning, etc.)?

- Screening facilities?

- Basic compliment of camera, sound, and other equipment?

- Use of casting facilities?

This list is not exhaustive but presents the types of questions that should be asked during negotiations.

Although the overhead rate may not ordinarily be negotiable, there are times when it in fact may be negotiated lower. If the principal photography is to be performed at a distant location where the facilities and services ordinarily provided by the studio are paid for and charged separately to the production, it would be appropriate to request a reduction in the contractual overhead rate. For instance, one of the authors was retained to assist in negotiations for an animated feature-length motion picture to be produced completely off the studio facility. The studio/financier agreed to a significantly reduced overhead charge due to these circumstances.

Presumably, the overhead rate is computed to absorb all of the studio's costs that are not directly charged to a picture given a certain rate of facilities usage. It will serve no purpose here to discuss the differences between the contractual rate and the actual cost. There may be a substantial difference and, maybe, there should be. The studio—with its blacksmiths; sign painters; lumber mill; soundstages; laborers; transportation equipment; prop, costumes, and supplies inventories; electrical shop; etc.—has a huge annual cost. If this contractual overhead rate is required to support the studio operation, it might be justified. (Or was the facilities charge and the supplemental labor cost rate designed to support the studio operation?)

PARTICIPATIONS IN GROSS BEFORE BREAKEVEN

All participations are discussed at length in the Participations section of this book. However, because a number of major distributor/financiers include amounts paid to participants prior to breakeven plus contractual overhead as part of the cost of production, these should be mentioned in this section on Production Cost.

Certain major talent (actors, directors, etc.) can obtain a participation in gross (as defined) as explained in the Participation section, commencing at various stages during the distribution. Frequently, such a person will receive an advance (during the production period) recoupable against a participation earned from the first dollar of receipts. If, for example, an actor received an advance of $5 million against a participation in gross receipts (as defined) and breakeven occurred when those defined gross receipts reached $50 million, the participation in gross before breakeven would be only the amount ($5 million) advanced during the production.

Breakeven is another concept to be discussed more fully under the Participations section, but for purposes of discussion here, breakeven occurs when gross receipts equal distribution fees, distribution expenses, and production costs, including interest. And the term "breakeven" relates, in this situation, to the definition of net profits for a particular net-profit participant. It is possible to have different net-profit definitions for different net-profit participants, and each could have a different amount of participation in net profits (as defined) before breakeven.

Confused?

Let's try an example. Assume a $10 million production cost, 5% participation in gross before breakeven, and $10 million of distribution expenses. Participant #1 negotiated a 15% overall distribution fee and Participant #2 negotiated a 35% overall distribution fee (a little absurd, but necessary for this example).

This is how the fee affects the receipts necessary to reach breakeven:

AT BREAKEVEN

	Participant #1	Participant #2
Receipts	$25,000,000	$33,333,333
Distribution Fee @ 15%	3,750,000	————
Distribution Fee @ 35%	————	11,666,666
Distribution Expense	10,000,000	10,000,000
Production Cost	10,000,000	10,000,000
Gross Participation @ 5%	1,250,000	1,666,667
Net Profit/Breakeven	0	0

Observe how Participant #1 reached breakeven with only $25 million in receipts, while Participant #2 requires $33.3 million to reach the same point. (The above example ignores overhead on participations before breakeven.) Distribution fees *matter*.

Participations in gross receipts, which are deductible as production costs and carry additional contractual overhead, are an increasing problem for writers and other talent, who can only negotiate a net profit deal. As more and more talent negotiate participations in gross receipts and as higher costs (production and distribution) result in higher breakeven points, the net profit participant is seeing less and less contingent compensation.

This is the type of problem encountered by Art Buchwald in his suit against Paramount Pictures. Although *Coming to America* had gross receipts of approximately $125 million, it still had a deficit of $18 million under Buchwald's net profit formula. However, it would take an additional $44 million in gross receipts in order to cover the deficit, as follows:

Gross Receipts	$44,000,000
Distribution Fee	13,000,000
Participations in	
Gross Receipts	
@ 25%	11,000,000
Overhead @ 15%	2,000,000
	18,000,000
Deficit	(18,000,000)
Breakeven	0

INTEREST

Just as in most financing, a motion picture financed by a major studio/financier or studio/distributor/financier carries an interest charge. Although interest charges are more fully discussed in this book's Financing and Interest chapter, mention must be made here also because interest is often included as a deduction on the participation statement. Such accounting treatment is consistent with generally accepted accounting principals (FASB #53), amazing as that may sound.

Unfortunately, the net profit participant often forgets about the effect interest can have in delaying his participation. This is all the more true when the receipts are slow in coming in, such as in episodic television programs. This may be one of the major reasons why Fess Parker has yet to see any net profits from the *Daniel Boone* series.

Interest is charged by the major distributor/financiers at the following rates:

- Paramount: 125% x prime rate of the Chemical Bank of New York

- Warner Bros.: 125% x prime rate of the First National Bank of Boston

- Columbia Pictures: 125% x prime rate "by banks from which Columbia is then receiving financing in connection with the production of motion pictures."

- Walt Disney Pictures: 125% of the prime rate of Bank of America

- Universal Pictures: 125% of the prime rate ". . . charged by United States banks at the respective times at which interest is computed hereunder . . ."

The major distributors only charge interest on the unrecouped amount of production cost. Unrecouped distribution expenses are not subject to an interest charge, though distribution expenses do reduce the amount available to recoup outstanding production costs. Paramount and Disney charge interest on the aggregate of unrecouped direct charges, gross participations before breakeven, and overhead. They do not charge overhead on interest.

DEFERMENTS

For tax and other reasons, some talent may accept a deferment in lieu of payment during production. Although the circumstances requiring the payment of a deferment (deferral) can vary based upon the negotiations and the resulting contractual provisions, generally one type is contingent (such as the picture going into profits) and the other type is not contingent (maybe only dependent on the passage of time). In neither case is it appropriate for the distributor to include the amount of the unpaid deferment in the cost of production for the purposes of computing interest on unrecouped costs. In determining the breakeven point for the motion picture, it would be appropriate to include the noncontingent type of deferment in the production cost and, depending on the contractual provisions, it may also be appropriate to add on an overhead factor. Now, is it proper to compute interest on the amount of overhead added due to the non-contingent deferment? The contingent deferment, depending on the contractual provisions, is probably not subject to the overhead add-on.

Deferments, even though payable out of the first net profits, are paid before any participation is computed and paid to net profit participants. If the net profits are insufficient to pay 100% of all of the deferments, the contracts usually stipulate that each deferment should be paid *pari passu* (with equal pace). As an example, assume that at the time of the first accounting on *Power Lunch* net profits were only $50,000. The director was supposed to receive a deferment out of first net profits of $75,000. This deferment was to be paid *pari passu* with the $50,000 deferment payable to the writer.

The initial portion of the deferments paid would be computed as follows:

Director: $50,000 x $75,000/$125,000   = $30,000

Writer: $50,000 x $50,000/$125,000   = $20,000

Total Deferments Paid $50,000

Even though this type of deferment is payable out of net profits, the participant in net profits will participate after the deduction of deferments. So a net profit participant would not participate in the $50,000 in the above example.

CONCLUSION

Production costs are a common area for audit claims and disputes between the distributor/studio/financier and the profit participant.

The wise profit participant knows this, and takes care to address potential disputes by careful advance negotiating. Remember, in motion picture participations, the key is the definition.

Knowledge about how a theatrical picture is made can be invaluable for the participant. As for everything in participations, knowledge is often power, which can translate into cash.

Chapter Seven

PARTICIPATIONS

When Art Buchwald took on Paramount Pictures over his participation in *Coming to America*, the world got a rare public glimpse of the inner workings of motion picture profit participations.

The court record is filled with testimony by the top experts of the late 1980s, speaking their minds in favor of and against the participations system that existed then, and exists today. One Paramount witness was Mel Sattler, a former studio vice president and, for more than twenty years, executive in charge of the business affairs department at Universal Pictures for feature motion pictures worldwide. While testifying for Paramount, Mr. Sattler recited a detailed history of motion picture participations that bears repeating:

Until the 1950s, the "studio system" governed the relationship between the major motion-picture studios and talent. The studios hired performers on an exclusive basis and paid them a fixed weekly or per-picture salary. In very rare cases, performers were given percentages of so-called "profit" pools contingent on the success of a motion picture. A few directors and producers were able to bargain on an ad hoc basis for "backend" deals—the right to a percentage of the studio's rentals of a particular motion picture after the studio recovered its distribution fee, distribution expenses, and production costs.

Jimmy Stewart's 1950 contract with Universal Pictures for the picture *Winchester '73* marks the emergence of the modern-day "participation." Stewart, then a major talent, commanded $200,000 to $250,000 in fixed "up front" compensation per picture, which was beyond the financial reach of Universal. (The studio had suffered a string of unsuccessful pictures and was in financial straits.) For reasons not germane here, to make a deal, Stewart's agent (Lew Wasserman, whose company, MCA, coincidentally, later acquired the studio), proposed an arrangement that in lieu of Stewart's fixed "up-front" compensation, Stewart would receive a 50% share of the "Net Profits" (defined as the point at which the motion picture earned in "Gross Receipts"—as defined in his contract—twice its negative cost, or in other words, a contractually defined "breakeven").

Universal accepted the proposal because it permitted the company to put substantially less at risk by reducing its immediate production costs. So-called "Net Profit" deals were thus borne of a studio's desire for risk-reduction. I might point out that this arrangement was unique in another important respect which quickly disappeared—if the motion picture never reached breakeven, Stewart received *nothing* for his services. He thus shared a portion of the risk in the production of the motion picture—his "compensation."

So-called "net profits" deals soon ceased being a way to share the risk of failure and instead became a way for performers to share only the rewards of success. By the mid-1950s, talent representatives were demanding that "net profits" be paid in addition to, and not in lieu of, "up-front" fixed compensation. The studios acceded, but soon found themselves bound by deals that called for "up-front" cash payments and "backend" compensation that drained the revenues from successful motion pictures which were necessary to finance the studios' customary development programs and slate of motion pictures.

In the market-driven balancing of risks and rewards, the studios began insisting on and receiving terms that increased the amount of revenue necessary to reach "breakeven" in the computation of "net profits." For example, distribution fees—the "sales commission" the studio deducts from gross receipts to finance the organization that sees to it that its motion picture are booked and exhibited—increased. Interest charges were levied on the money both borrowed and advanced for production costs. Collectively, these modifications assured the studio a larger share of the revenues generated by "hit" movies to compensate them for the losses they sustained on "disasters."

So-called "gross" deals quickly emerged as a reaction to counter this reallocation of benefits. By the early 1960s, the top stars (and a handful of directors) demanded not only increasingly large up-front payments, but more often a share of the receipts before the studio deducted its distribution fee.

The father of the "net profit" deal, Jimmy Stewart, was soon receiving $250,000 plus 10% of the "gross."

The balance of rewards on both so-called "gross" and "net" contingent-compensation deals began shifting markedly toward participants during the late 1970s and early 1980s when independent production companies—such as Melvin Simon Productions, The Ladd Company, Polygram, Lorimar, and Cannon Pictures—began competing for creative talent. In order to establish themselves, these "independents" offered generous compensation packages (which included large up-front payments and contingent compensation) to well-known actors, writers, and directors. Compounding these forces, the studios expanded production to meet the demand from new markets and media. The increase in film production unavoidably created sharp competition for the scarce box-office draws, who were now more frequently able to command "gross" rather than "net" deals.

By 1983, the major stars and directors were commanding anywhere from 5%, based upon a graduating scale of "gross receipts," to 12½ or 15% of a motion picture.

GROSS RECEIPTS

FADE IN:

INT. OFFICE — DUSK

Bernie gazes through the window at the sun
setting in the distant Pacific Ocean.

Bernie turns his attention to his computer
screen. Sharon's chin rests lightly on
Bernie's shoulder as she follows his work.
David is massaging Jennifer's shoulders as
they rest from their sorting chores; she
lets out a contented sigh.

Suddenly, Bernie straightens and whoops,
clapping his hands together. Sharon is
startled, grabbing his waist to steady
herself.

                    BERNIE
          Ah-hah! I gotcha!

David and Jennifer hurry over to see what
he is talking about. Sharon is tightly
focused on the computer display. Her face
flushes with concern.

                    SHARON
                (evenly)
            That bastard.

David and Jennifer crowd around the
screen.

                    DAVID
            What is it?

                    BERNIE
            Just what I suspected, only with
            a twist.

He stands and stretches, yawning.

                    BERNIE
            Sylvester Sturdy is the culprit,
            naturally. He is getting a first-
            dollar gross deal that cuts the
            heart out of Sharon's deal. That
            shouldn't be such a surprise.

                    SHARON
                (angrily)
            It's a surprise to me! That
            s.o.b. brought squat to Power
            Lunch. And now you tell me
            he's going to get rich and I'm
            getting the proverbial shaft?

Bernie grins knowingly.

                    DAVID
               (slowly)
          I don't think that's what
          he means.

                    BERNIE
               (brightly)
          You know what, David, you're
          right! Sharon, what you just
          described is exactly what
          usually happens when a net-
          profit participant works in a
          picture where there is a major
          first-dollar participation deal
          in place. Only this isn't your
          usual deal.

                    SHARON
               (hopefully)
          It's not?

                    BERNIE
          Would I lie to you?

                    SHARON
               (cautiously)
          How long have you been in
          the business?

                              FADE OUT

THE DEALS

Certain stars command "first-dollar gross" deals that earn them as much as $25 million per motion picture, typically paid as an up-front advance against a healthy share of the "gross." These participations begin paying from the commencement of distribution.

Those deals are for talent who lives at the very top of the food chain. Mere mortals don't have things quite so jolly.

Instead, the vast majority of the world participates on a percentage basis after some arithmetic breakeven formula is satisfied. Understanding what the percentage represents and how breakeven is achieved is what makes profit participations simultaneously so intriguing and aggravating.

UNDERSTANDING THE TERMINOLOGY

The first thing to recognize is that if the talent gets, say "15 points," it could mean many things. For example, 15% of the adjusted gross receipts typically represents a number one-third greater than 15% of net profits under the usual studio formula. But that's only the typical case; what the terms actually mean in the context of any given deal will depend entirely upon the controlling contractual provisions and definitions.

Likewise, terms such as gross receipts, exclusions, distribution fees, distribution expenses, production costs, and net profits may vary somewhat from producer to producer, and it isn't unusual that these same terms may also vary in each contract from the same producer. This is interesting to note, because the motion picture industry has a general consensus as to what those terms mean.

Other terms are used just as frequently (e.g., adjusted gross, true gross, cash breakeven, and actual breakeven) that are also contractually defined terms, but for which there is *no* consensus within the industry as to their precise definition.

The lesson is, READ THE CONTRACT. The terms in motion picture profit participations are *always* defined.

Knowledgeable players understand the game. Indeed, the story goes that when John Wayne was signed by Universal to star in the motion picture *Rooster Cogburn*, his representatives insisted that Universal incorporate a copy of the studio's net profit definition from a generation before as controlling terms in the newer deal. Since that older definition had been first issued, Universal had revised and revamped their Exhibit "A" innumerable times. Presumably, Mr. Wayne and his representatives believed that the studio's revisions probably were not intended to benefit actors signing up for new roles.

THE AGREEMENTS

Profit participation agreements are generally extremely complex documents. This is understandable, since they have evolved into delicately balanced formulas after years of bargaining, practice, and recalculating by studios and talent representatives alike. As a result, in standard profit-participation agreements, the so-called "Exhibit 'A'" definition to every talent contract is generally an obtuse, difficult document that even the studio's own negotiating attorney might not understand. Since only a few individuals at any studio would be willing to risk tampering with an Exhibit "A" formula, the hopelessly arcane is often the standardized form. This can lead to some practical problems.

Although an Exhibit "A" provision may seem fairly easy to understand to the agent or attorney, it may be ambiguous or impossible when the accountant tries to apply it to the actual financial transactions. Both the provisions of the contract and the intention behind those provisions are subject to interpretation by the accountant. Since reasonable interpretations may vary, there is often lots to talk about in a dispute over film proceeds.

TALENT AGREEMENTS

The most common contemporary talent agreement is actually an employment contract specifically tailored to the motion picture business. Producers, directors, and talent are essentially hired as studio employees and attached to specific projects. They create works for hire that are wholly owned by the contracting studio. In return, they are paid fixed and contingent compensation. The latter includes participating in the "backend" profits.

These deals tend to be quite formulaic, which is understandable because they are the basic contracts that the motion picture industry utilizes for creating its product. Generally speaking, talent is free to negotiate its best deal on the terms within the basic contract itself, but the Exhibit "A"-defined terms are off-limits for all but the most powerful players.

Not to say that definitions can never be negotiated. But generally speaking, they can't be and they aren't. Still, when a film hits at the box office and the money is pouring in, participants are free to assert their audit rights and challenge inequities in the definitions. Audits followed by claims are a time-honored tradition in the motion picture business, and they can and do justify their expense.

"HOLLYWOOD ACCOUNTING"

Another practice often works against the participant, and this practice is so notorious or infamous that it has entered the popular lexicon.

Mention "Hollywood Accounting" to most any person on the street and they will likely understand you as referring to a system that cheats talent, bilks them out of their hard-earned profits, and then smilingly invites them out to a nice lunch in a fancy restaurant. But not everyone believes this is actually the case.

The often-maligned accounting practices of the motion picture industry are only the practices and interpretations required by the provisions of a contract that is usually freely negotiated by a knowledgeable studio attorney on one side and a knowledgeable talent representative on the other.

When a transaction that is not spelled out in the contract occurs, each of the parties may be expected to take a position (interpretation relative to the accounting treatment) that is most beneficial to themselves. These opposing positions are normally negotiated (based upon relative power at the time) and lawsuits seldom result.

Even so, a healthy mythology surrounding profit participation contracts and Hollywood accounting continually feeds public skepticism about the entire system. One of the authors remembers how one of his mentors swore up and down that Universal kept no fewer than five sets of books for any given production. One of the other authors was a high executive at Universal during this same period and swears equally strongly that only a single set of books was kept for any given purpose, so that anecdote may be more illustrative of motion picture studio mystique than Hollywood accounting technique.

The Distribution Agreement

The major studio can be a one-stop movie shop, serving as producer, financier, facilities lessor, and film distributor. However, a studio *need* not be all those things for every project. In recent times, a brand of deep-pocketed entrepreneurs have utilized their own capital to produce films that are then distributed through a major studio's distribution system.

Needless to say, the less you need from a major studio, the more you might be able to negotiate in your participation deal.

Deal structures vary as widely as the movies they precipitate. Ideas, concepts, and treatments are presented to studios by the hundreds each week. What a studio will pay for one undeveloped script is significantly less than if the screenplay is part of a project with a well-known actor and/or director attached. If all the pieces are in place, a producer might go so far as to approach a studio with a completed motion picture seeking only distribution. The more pieces the producer controls, the more leverage there is in a deal—assuming, of course, the film is attracting interest in the marketplace.

Star Vehicle in the Can

Starting with the highest leverage position, assume a producer approaches the studio with a completed motion picture, including well-known talent, funds for releasing costs, and worldwide rights intact. The studio will be concerned with whether the motion picture has any commercial potential, but most will probably be willing to talk about a distribution deal.

In this sort of scenario, the producer has a blank paper upon which can be structured all kinds of deals. The producing company might well be able to negotiate a deal in which it receives 82.5% of the gross receipts from first dollar, with the studio retaining 17.5% as its distribution fee.

Sample 82.5%/17.5% split:

Gross Receipts $100,000,000

82.5% Share $82,500,000 (to the producing company)

17.5% Share $17,500,000 (to the distributor)

Even so, it may be that the producer financed the motion picture's releasing costs with an investor who demanded a priority position from all film revenues. In that case, although the distributor might agree to a priority position for recoupment of the releasing costs, the distributor might then demand a 20% distribution fee from first dollar, payable after recoupment of releasing costs. The distributor justifies this extra 2.5% fee because it is not participating from the first dollar as it would if the investor had not required priority. The numbers break down like this:

	1st Month	1st Quarter	Ultimate
Gross Receipts	$15,000,000	$60,000,000	$100,000,000
Distribution Fee	2,500,000	12,000,000	20,000,000
Releasing Costs	12,500,000	25,000,000	32,500,000
Remainder Available to Producer	$0	$23,000,000	$47,500,000

Note that in this example, the distributor did not get its full distribution fee (20% x $15,000,000 = $3,000,000) in the first month of release because the releasing costs had a priority recoupment position. The risk to the distributor is that it *never* earns its full fee if the picture bombs. Hence the extra 2.5%.

If the producer could have accepted a *parri passu* (instead of priority) position with the distributor and negotiated an 82.5% interest, he would have received $12,375,000 or $125,000 less. However, in order to obtain the priority recoupment, it cost the producer $2,500,000 (80% vs. 82.5% of $100,000,000).

Another way of achieving the same end might be to obtain a guarantee. For example, the producer might obtain a guarantee from the distributor equal to the initial releasing costs. Because the distributor still has all rights, worldwide, it might be willing to give such a guarantee at a minimal cost to the producer (maybe a half a point or an 18% distribution fee instead of a 17.5% one). However, in this instance the financier of the releasing costs must understand the business and the security of its investment.

A canny financier might require more in compensation from the producer for the use of funds to finance the releasing costs.

PRE-SELLING RIGHTS

To finance the releasing costs or even a portion of the production costs, the producer might carve out some of the distribution rights and pre-sell these. A common practice for independent financing is to presell the foreign rights through a foreign sales agent (see the discussion above). The downside is that when the producer approaches the domestic distributor, it has less than a whole pie to sell, which may affect the value of that deal. Still, pre-sales continue to constitute an important source for production dollars because they provide a means for funding a picture without studio dollars up front.

Depending on the perceived, potential, commercial success of the theatrical motion picture in the domestic marketplace, the domestic distributor still might be willing to offer a very favorable deal to the producer (maybe a 22.5% distribution fee) even if certain key territorial rights are pre-sold.

The general rule is that as the producer continues to carve out and pre-sell distribution rights, the value of the remaining rights decreases.

NEGATIVE PICK-UP DISTRIBUTION DEAL

In a negative pick-up distribution deal (the "negative" in this case being *film* negative), a producer controlling all domestic rights will make a deal with a studio for distribution only. Typically, in this sort of deal, the distributor finances releasing costs and provides an advance against the distribution results to the producer.

The advantage to the studio is that the producer risks the production capital, limiting the studio's risk to distribution. The disadvantage to the studio is that when the film is a runaway smash hit, the upside is limited because its income from the picture is limited to the distribution fee.

Auditman, a modern day Robin Hood tale about a participation auditor, was a negative pick-up, produced with independent money but distributed through a major. The distribution deal had some key requirements.

The foreign distribution pre-sale commitments required that *Auditman* had to open on at least 1,000 domestic screens supported by a minimum of $5 million in prints and advertising spending.

When the deal came to the studio, it estimated the film was worth a minimum of $15 million in gross receipts and potentially as much as $50 million. However, the studio also estimated it would cost at least $10 million in prints and advertising costs to distribute the picture.

	Minimum	Potential
Theatrical Film Rental	$5,000,000	$26,000,000
Home Video Royalty	5,000,000	12,000,000
Television	5,000,000	12,000,000
Total Estimated Gross Receipts	15,000,000	50,000,000
Distribution Expenses	10,000,000	20,000,000
Est. Net Distribution Results Before Distribution Fee	$5,000,000	$30,000,000

So, two questions remained: How much of a distribution fee could the studio request (how low could they afford to go), and how much of a distribution advance must they offer?

Based upon the above estimates, prudence would dictate that the studio should not offer less than a 25% distribution fee and a maximum $1 to $2 million advance. However, if the studio was fairly confident that gross receipts would be at least $20 million, based upon this particular picture, they might be willing to risk more of an advance. Still, it would be not be prudent to offer more than a $5 million advance, because that is the maximum net result from the low-end earning estimate. Also, where cutting the distribution fee would be inconsistent with other deals the studio negotiated previously with other parties, there could be a complication if any of the other contracts contain "most favored nations" clauses that automatically give them the best terms in any studio contract.

This is where the number-crunchers go to work:

BREAKEVEN FOR STUDIO AT A 25% FEE AND A $5 MILLION ADVANCE

Distribution Expenses	$10 million
Advance to Producer	5 million
Total Monies at Risk	15 million
Distribution Fee @ 25%	(divide by .75)
Breakeven Gross Receipts =	$20 million

A financier might look at the above computation and not understand why someone would risk $15 million for only a $5 million profit or a potential loss. So it's important to understand that this calculation only works where the studio is reasonably confident that the breakeven point is nearly a sure thing, and that in all probability it represents a *minimum* estimate of the film's potential.

(Another important financial matter, not shown here but certainly considered if the distributor intends on staying in business, is the time it will take to recoup the studio investment and earn the distribution fee.)

CO-PRODUCTION/DISTRIBUTION DEALS

There are non-profit reasons for entering into co-production deals. A producer may wish to retain control of a property but lack the financing to complete its production. The distributor may wish to invest only enough to obtain rights to a limited number of territories. The producer may wish to hold back certain territories for its own account, selling off only enough rights to have the picture produced, and then rely on a negative pick-up deal to take care of domestic distribution.

One of the most innovative financing structures of its time was the deal that financed *Green Card*, starring the French superstar (in France, anyway) Gérard Depardieu and Andie MacDowell.

At the time, Depardieu was relatively unknown in the U.S. market, but a major sensation abroad. Using Depardieu's box-office appeal in the foreign markets, his attorney, Nigel Sinclair, and agent, John Ptak (then with William Morris, currently at CAA), skillfully sold off just enough foreign territories and other rights to produce the picture, holding back as much as possible for the producers and their client, director Peter Weir. Domestic distribution was through Disney on a negative pick-up deal.

The picture did moderately well in the States, and was strong around the world. But because of the financing structure, *Green Card* is still bandied about in Hollywood as being one of *the* most financially successful pictures of its day for the creative talent.

But most co-productions are substantially less complex than the *Green Card* model. A typical deal might be to share the production cost between two distributors, with Distributor A handling the domestic territory (U.S. and Canada) and Distributor B distributing in the foreign territories. (The following examples ignore outside participations and combine all receipts, regardless of media or market, for simplicity's sake.) *Titanic* followed this model, with Fox handling foreign and Paramount handling domestic distribution. Both were left drowning in a green sea of cash.

	Total	Dist. A	Dist. B
THE FAILURE:			
Total Receipts	$18,000,000	$10,000,000	$8,000,000
Dist. Fee @ 30%/40%	6,200,000	3,000,000	3,200,000
Balance	11,800,000	7,000,000	4,800,000
Dist. Expenses	5,400,000	3,000,000	2,400,000
Balance	6,400,000	4,000,000	2,400,000
Production Cost	20,000,000	10,000,000	10,000,000
Loss on Picture	(13,600,000)	(6,000,000)	(7,600,000)
Add Back Dist. Fee	6,200,000	3,000,00	3,200,000
Loss on Deal	$(7,400,000)	$(3,000,000)	$(4,400,000)

THE SUCCESS:

Total Receipts	$63,000,000	$35,000,000	$28,000,000
Dist. Fee @ 30%/40%	21,700,000	10,500,000	11,200,000
Balance	41,300,000	24,500,000	16,800,000
Dist. Expenses	13,500,000	7,500,000	6,000,000
Balance	27,800,000	17,000,000	10,800,000
Production Cost	20,000,000	10,000,000	10,000,000
Profit on Picture	7,800,000	7,000,000	800,000
Add Back Dist. Fee	21,700,000	10,500,000	11,200,000
Profit on Deal	$29,500,000	$17,500,000	$12,000,000

The above examples were computed using an 80% factor for the foreign distribution results, that is, foreign receipts are assumed to equal 80% of the domestic receipt total. That number can vary widely. In today's market, foreign often is at least as important as domestic in gross dollars, while some pictures have far greater foreign appeal than domestic. On the other hand, some genres, as a rule, don't travel well. Comedies usually do far better in the domestic marketplace, though some performers manage to break that rule. Jerry Lewis's god-like status in France is an example, though the phenomenon baffles many even to this day. So is the *Look Who's Talking* series, where each of the sequels were hits overseas while performing relatively modestly domestically.

In the above chart, the same 80% ratio was used for foreign distribution expenses, although this may also not necessarily hold true. The distribution fees have been computed exactly at 30% for domestic and 40% for foreign, although this might vary depending upon the source of the receipts (i.e., theatrical, home video, television, etc.).

Today, a $20 million production cost is a fairly small picture, and worldwide film rental of $63 million isn't that great, either. Still, all things are relative, and a $63 million gross on a $20 million picture is a happy result.

TALENT NET AND GROSS PARTICIPATIONS

WHAT IT IS

Net profit participations are not and never have been a share of the studio/financier/distributor's profits. Nor were they ever intended to be.

While a performer or other creative artist may well incur a career risk on any given film—the saying goes, "You're only as good as your last picture," and your compensation on future projects is generally tied to the performance of your last film—the participant (usually) assumes no capital risk. On the capital side, at most, the participant risks services (and this seldom occurs in today's world) for a reduction in direct compensation that might otherwise be paid.

The participation in net profits is a contractually defined formula by which a participant might obtain additional compensation if various criteria are met. Now, there is a general sense that Hollywood net profits are a sham, and that no net profit participant ever sees a dime from their participations deal. The fact that Eddie Murphy (a gross player, by the way) felt free to deride net points as "monkey points" during the *Coming to America* (aka Buchwald) case is simple testament to the conventional wisdom that net points are good for cocktail-party conversation and little else.

Even so, the defined criteria in net profit definitions are indeed sometimes met; the idea that a participation in net profits is "an impossible dream" is not true.

Paramount tried to make that point in the Buchwald case, where its witnesses testified that "twenty-nine of the motion pictures released by Paramount from 1975 to 1988 achieved significant net profits—an annual average of more than two of the studio's fifteen releases. These films paid out to over eighty-four profit participants more than $155 million."

But in recent years, there is no question that net participants have seen their chances of earning a contingent dollar dwindling away as strong players in the industry take ever larger *gross* profit shares from pictures.

NET VERSUS GROSS

Talent (an actor, a director, a writer, etc.) may participate in net profits as contractually defined, or in gross receipts as contractually defined, depending upon what they are perceived as bringing to a project. This perception of bringing value, be it drawing an audience or attracting other key talent, is what is generally referred to in the industry as "clout." The simple rule: Clout matters.

"As contractually defined" is all important in determining the amount of contingent compensation the talent might receive, whether the participation is in net profits, gross receipts, or some variation on either theme.

For example, in this book we generally accept that net profits are defined as: Gross Receipts, less (1) Distribution Fees, (2) Distribution Expenses, and (3) Production Costs, the latter of which may include overhead, interest, and participations in gross receipts.

If there is a deferment "payable out of first net profits," then the net profit for the net profit participant is computed after the deduction of the deferment(s) paid.

Participations in gross receipts before breakeven are usually deducted from the preliminary net profit amount in order to compute the net profits upon which the net profit participant's share is based.

Frequently, a contractual overhead is added to the participation in gross receipts in arriving at net profits. For purposes of simplification, this was not done in arriving at net profits in the computation for *Power Lunch*.

Net Profit Before Participation	$16,000,000
Less Deferments Paid	125,000
Participation in Gross	6,875,000
Total	7,000,000
Net Profit after Participation	$9,000,000

If 15% overhead on participations in gross receipts before breakeven had been charged, the net profit after participation would have been reduced $1,031,250 (15% x $6,875,000).

Additionally, many net profit formulas (contractual provisions) allow deduction of third-party participations after breakeven. For example, Paragraph I. of the Paramount Pictures Net Profit Definition - Exhibit "A":

I. APPLICATION OF GROSS RECEIPTS

Gross Receipts shall be applied to the following categories on a continuing basis and in the herein listed order of priority:

A. Fees . . .

B. Expenses . . .

C. Other Participations

Amounts PPC may be contractually obligated to pay (whether as a deferment other than those specified in E below), a gross receipts participation, or otherwise, but excluding any sums payable by way of net profit participations which come out of the Participant's share of net profits (as may be provided in this agreement) to any person including Participant, but excluding any share of net profits payable to Participant or PPC hereunder, for rights or services in connection with Picture, based or dependent on all or any part of percentage of the gross receipts (whether or not such gross receipts are defined or computed in the same manner as set forth herein) and which are not included in the computation of negative cost, are called participations. In computing share of Participant hereunder, a participation shall be deductible hereunder (not withstanding the order of priority in this Paragraph I) if, when and to the extent that PPC obligation to pay it accrues, whether or not such payment has then become due or been made and regardless of whether PPC has recovered its negative cost.

D. Negative Cost . . .

E. Deferments

All amounts payable pursuant to a contract approved in writing by PPC to any person entitled to same out of first net profits or immediately prior to there being such net profits, provided such amounts shall not be a percentage of net profits, unless there is a different order of payment specified under this agreement.

F. Net Profits

Net profits are the gross receipts, if any, remaining after deduction of items specified in Paragraph A through E inclusive.

Such language, if not amended through negotiations, raises the specter of a picture with two separate net participations (say a 5% and a 10% net profit participation), which are deductible from each other in arriving at net profits. So, how do you do that?

This is an algebraic equation and may be expressed as follows:

$$P1 = 5\% \times (\text{Net Profits} - P2)$$
$$P2 = 10\% \times (\text{Net Profits} - P1)$$

Solving for P1:

$$P1 = 5\% \times (\text{Net Profits} - 10\% \times (\text{Net Profits} - P1))$$

or

$$.995 \times P1 = .045 \times \text{Net Profits}$$

Assuming Net Profits before participations of $1 million:

$$P1 = \$45,226$$
$$P2 = \$95,477$$

Frequently, this contractual provision is amended. For example, the "rider" to Exhibit "A" to the agreement between Paramount Pictures Corporation and Boccodor Enterprises, Inc., f/s/o (for the services of) Art Buchwald contained the following language in Paragraph 1:

With respect to paragraph I.C., the following provision shall be added as the last sentence: "Notwithstanding the foregoing to the contrary, third-party net profit participations shall not be deductible under this paragraph."

GROSS RECEIPTS

Some major talent (actors, directors, and a few writers) can command a participation in the gross receipts of a motion picture. Even so, the term "gross receipts" has more than one contractual definition in a motion picture.

The definition of gross receipts for computing net profits includes certain receipts and excludes certain receipts. The definition of gross receipts for a participation in gross receipts includes the same definition (inclusions and exclusions), but also allows deductions for certain "off-the-top" expenses.

In director John Landis's contract for a participation in gross receipts from *Coming to America*, the following off-the-top deductions were specified:

(1) Conversion

Costs, discounts, and expenses incurred in obtaining remittances of receipts to the U.S., including costs of contesting imposition of restricted funds.

(2) Checking

Checking theater attendance and receipts and investigating unauthorized usage of Picture, whether payable to or incurred by PPC employees or other persons. Added by Rider: "but deduction of such costs shall not exceed 1% of the Gross Receipts of the Picture."

(3) Collections

Costs incurred in connection with collection of Gross Receipts, including attorney and auditor fees and costs and liability incurred by PPC in connection therewith.

(4) <u>Residuals</u>

Residuals are costs incurred and payments required under applicable collective-bargaining agreements by reason of or as a condition to use or exhibition of Picture in television or any other media. To extent such payments are made to or on behalf of Participant, such payments shall be deemed a credit against any percentage compensation payable to Participant hereunder to extent not prohibited by the applicable collective-bargaining agreement. Any payments made to Participant hereunder prior to payment of residuals are deemed a credit against such residuals to extent not prohibited by applicable collective-bargaining agreement. In neither event may credit, when applicable, be deducted a second time against Participant.

(Note: This paragraph was amended by the following language in the agreement: "Notwithstanding anything to the contrary contained elsewhere, PPC shall not credit or offset residuals or supplemental market payments against Lender's[1] participation hereunder or vice-versa.")

(5) <u>Trade Dues</u>

Allocable portion of dues, assessments, including legal fees and costs and contributions to MPAA, AMPTP, or similarly constituted or substitute organization throughout the world (including legal fees to counsel respecting antitrust matters and matters formerly handled by AMPTP prior to PPC's withdrawal therefrom).

(Note: Added by Rider, "up to a maximum of $75,000 and there shall be excluded fees of PPC in-house counsel.")

(6) <u>Licenses</u>

---

[1] "Lender" refers to Landis's loan-out corporation.

All licenses, duties, fees, or any other amounts required to permit use of Picture.

(7) <u>Taxes</u>

Taxes and governmental fees of any nature and however characterized, including costs of contesting, interest, and penalties thereon (other than PPC or subdistributor corporate income taxes), imposed directly or indirectly on Picture or any part thereof (including without limitation the Employer's share of payroll taxes with respect to deferred or contingent compensation) or on the Gross Receipts or the license, distribution, or exhibition of Picture or collection, conversion, or remittance of monies connected therewith.

(Note: Added by Rider, "excluding fees of PPC in-house counsel.")

(8) <u>Theater Level Advertising</u>

"Theater Level Advertising Expenses" shall mean all payments made, sums expended, or credits allowed by PPC in connection with advertising and exploitation at the theater level (whether or not PPC shares with the exhibitor the cost of such advertising and exploitation). "Theater Level Advertising" shall include, but not be limited to, advertising in newspapers, on radio and television, personal appearances by actors and other production personnel in connection with or for the Picture, salaries and expenses of PPC's publicity advertising personnel and field exploitation men, all of which shall be appropriately allocated to the Picture to the extent that such expenses shall be paid or incurred in connection with advertising at the theater level.

(Note: In the Landis agreement, this paragraph was crossed out, as it is in virtually every gross agreement.)

The above not only shows the types of deductions made by distributors in computing gross receipts for participants in gross receipts, it also demonstrates the potential for amending the boilerplate contract definitions through negotiations.

What Gross Isn't

In the Hollywood mythology, some actors are so important that they receive a gross participation in the box-office receipts of the motion picture. But, in real life, if a producer were to negotiate such a deal, "heaven help him." In truth, even the "first-dollar gross" deal doesn't mean what the label implies.

First of all, the actor would be entitled to a share of an amount that the distributor did not receive, and which the exhibitor isn't about to give up. Secondly, due to rates of exchange and other factors, even the distributor may not accurately know the total box-office gross. So, who could compute the actor's participation if it truly were based solely on box-office receipts?

Another myth is that some actors are so important that they participate in the "true distributor gross." However, this myth is improbable from the start, because no one can even say what "true gross" is; in truth, "true gross" is not a commonly used Hollywood term. Still, myths die hard, and some will define the term "true gross" as meaning the same gross used in computing net profits, with all its inclusions and exclusions, but omitting the deductions.

Again, if this myth had some credibility (which has never been substantiated), the actor would be entitled to a share of an amount the distributor did not receive due to withholding taxes, collection costs, exchange rates, etc.

Sylvester Sturdy's representatives did not carefully negotiate all of the points in his participation in gross receipts. As shown below, both cooperative advertising (theater level advertising, which almost never is considered off-the-top) and taxes (which almost always are considered off-the-top) were defined as "off-the-top" deductions in computing the participation:

(in thousands)

	Before Break-even	After Break-even	Total
Gross Receipts	$45,000	$55,000	$100,000
Cooperative Adv.	10,000	10,000	20,000
Taxes	0	2,000	2,000
Total	10,000	12,000	22,000
Contractual Gross Receipts	$35,000	$43,000	$78,000
Participation Rate	10%	12.5%	
Participation	$3,500	$5,375	$8,875
Paid During Production			2,000
Additional Contingent Compensation			$6,875

BREAKEVEN

In many talent/producer/distributor/studio/financier contracts, a variety of things may occur at some magical number termed "breakeven." The rate (percentage share) of a participation may change (as in Sylvester Sturdy's deal) or it may begin; contractual overhead may no longer be applied against participations in net profits; calculations of interest may cease; etc. A classical accounting definition of breakeven would be when revenues equal deductions.

Not to be restricted by "classical accounting definitions," agents and attorneys (as well as the studio business-affairs folk) have concocted a myriad of definitions for breakeven. Whether these definitions are "dreamed up" in order to give their clients an advantage or to insure additional professional fees could be a subject of much discussion.

In order to show the complexity of these (even though the agents and attorneys may have thought them fairly simple and straightforward), we will discuss two examples. But, keep in mind, these are by no means the only deals in town.

ARTIFICIAL AND ACTUAL BREAKEVEN

The contractual provision may be along the lines of the following:

Talent gets 12.5% of gross receipts (ignoring off-the-top deductions, for this example) after actual breakeven. This is the same as net without a fee, and has the added practical effect of penalizing the other net participants (since the adjusted gross is charged against other net participations as an additional production expense and acts to further reduce net profits, if any). After the gross receipts reach 3.5 times production cost, talent gets another 2.5% (or 15% in total).[2]

	Actual Breakeven	Ultimate Net Profit
$5,000,000 PRODUCTION COST:		
Gross Receipts	$11,500,000	$50,000,000
Distribution Fee @ 30%	(3,450,000)	(15,000,000)
Distribution Expenses	(3,050,000)	(10,000,000)
Production Costs	(5,000,000)	(5,000,000)
Net Profit Before Part.	$0	$20,000,000
$10,000,000 PRODUCTION COST:		
Gross Receipts	$21,500,000	$50,000,000
Distribution Fee @ 30%	(6,450,000)	(15,000,000)
Distribution Expenses	(5,050,000)	(10,000,000)
Production Costs	(10,000,000)	(10,000,000)
Net Profit Before Part.	$0	$15,000,000

---

[2] Though the 3.5 times production-cost factor has fallen out of favor in the past decade.

PARTICIPATION COMPUTATIONS:

	$5,000,000 Production Cost	$10,000,000 Production Cost
Receipts at 3.5 Times Production Cost	$17,500,000	$35,000,000
Receipts at Actual Breakeven	11,500,000	21,500,000
Receipts Subject to 12.5% Participation	$6,000,000	$13,500,000
Ultimate Receipts	$50,000,000	$50,000,000
Receipts at 3.5 Times Production Cost	17,500,000	35,000,000
Receipts Subject to 15% Participation	$32,500,000	$15,000,000
Participation @ 12.5%	750,000	1,687,500
Participation @ 15.0%	4,875,000	2,250,000
Total	**$5,625,000**	**$3,937,500**
Net Profit After Participations	$14,375,000	$11,062,500

In the above example, it is interesting to note that although the production cost in one situation was $5 million more than the other situation, the net profit after participations was only $3,312,500 less ($14,375,000 minus $11,062,500).

Another way to look at this might be that the gross participant bore 33% of the increased production cost out of their participation. In negotiating the deal, representatives of both sides are (or should be) aware of all of these ramifications and have made projections of the "what ifs" during the negotiations.

This is one area in which an accountant familiar with participation computations *should be consulted.*

ROLLING BREAKEVEN

It may be that one dank morning, duly fueled by several potent "pick-me-ups," an inebriated attorney met with a demented accountant and, together, they developed the following:

Breakeven is the point at which revenues are equal to distribution fees, distribution expenses, and production costs *on a continuing basis.*

This can be illustrated as follows:

(in thousands)

	Initial Breakeven	Additional Expenses	New Breakeven
Gross Receipts	$10,000		$12,000
Distribution Fee @ 30%	3,000		3,600
Distribution Expenses	3,000	$1,400	4,400
Production Cost	4,000		4,000
Total	10,000		12,000
Net Profit	$0		$0

Since the rolling breakeven is normally used where an outside participant receives a share in gross receipts, is this really a participation in gross receipts or another way of computing a participation in net profits?

This is a fine point that would be important if another outside participant (such as Sylvester Sturdy in *Power Lunch*) had a deal that defined gross participations as a deduction from net profits, but did not allow a deduction for other third-party "net" participations.

Here the participant's accountant (auditor) might be justified in interpreting this as a net participation regardless of the contractual language, because net participations cannot be deducted from other nets, while adjusted gross participations can.

Producer's Share

The producer's share (participation) may be negotiated from a different perspective than the "additional compensation" viewpoint of the talent. The producer, to a greater or lesser extent, is responsible for the production of the motion picture, including all of the associated costs.

Therefore, logically, the producer should share in the cost of the talent in some manner, even if this cost is in the form of a participation paid long after the completion of the production. This may be accomplished by including third-party participations as a deduction in computing the producer's net profit.

For example, the computation of the producer share in *Power Lunch*:

Net Profit Before Participations	$16,000,000
Participations & Deferments	7,900,000
Net Profit After Participations	8,100,000
Producer Share @ 50%	4,050,000

In effect, the producer paid their 50% share of the $7,900,000 talent costs (or $3,950,000) out of their 50% share in the net profits.

Since the financier put up all of the money, they might think that they should get more than of the 50% of the profit after participations (if there was any), because they get 100% of any loss. If acceptable to the producer, the financier might have been able to negotiate a deal where the talent costs (in the form of participations) came directly out of the producer's share or:

Net Profit Before Participations	$16,000,000
Producer's Share @ 50%	8,000,000
Participations & Deferments	7,900,000
Producer's Participation	$100,000

Having projected the "what ifs" for this proposal, the producer might have countered with:

Producer is entitled to 50% of net profits, reducible to a minimum of 20% of net profits by third-party participations. Excess participations, if any, are taken off the top.

So far in this book, we have encountered "off-the-top" in computing distribution fee and in computing participations in gross receipts. The calculation for this proposal, using the *Power Lunch* factors and demonstrating the effect of taking excess participations off the top, is as follows:

First, we compute excess third-party participations, if there are any:

NET PROFITS BEFORE PARTICIPATIONS	$16,000,000
50% Producer's Share	8,000,000
Reducible by Third-Party Participations (and Deferments)	7,900,000
Difference	100,000
Minimum Producer's Share (20% x $16,000,000)	3,200,000
Excess Third-Party Participations	**$3,100,000**

Then, we deduct the excess third-party participations off-the-top:

NET PROFITS BEFORE PARTICIPATIONS	$16,000,000
Excess Third-Party Participations	3,100,000
Net Profit, Revised	**$12,900,000**

Then, we perform the first calculation based upon the revised net profit amount.

50% REVISED NET PROFITS	$6,450,000
Reducible by Third-Party Participations (and Deferments) After Deducting Excess ($7,900,000-$3,100,000)	4,800,000
DIFFERENCE	$1,650,000
MINIMUM PRODUCER SHARE @ 20% of Revised Net Profits, Which Is Greater Than 50% Share Reduced by Third-Party Participations	$2,580,000

There is still some controversy over the interpretation of the contractual phrase "x% of revised net profits, which is greater than the 50% share reduced by third-party participations." How many times should this calculation be made (continuing to deduct excess participations off of the top and arriving at a new revised net-profit amount)?

If the calculation was to be made with a heavy third-party participation burden, as in *Power Lunch*, the producer will always end up down at the hard floor.

Still, if that was the intention, then the contract provision should have been drafted to specifically say that.

PRODUCER PENALTIES

A number of contractual provisions can be used to penalize a producer (or a director) for allowing the production to go into an overbudget condition. The standard provision in the Paramount Pictures Net Profit Definition - Exhibit "A" (page 13, Paragraph V.D.) follows:

> An additional amount by which the cost of production exceeds the approved Picture budget by the lower of $300,000 or 10% of the budget shall be deemed included in cost of production, but such excess overbudget amounts shall not itself bear interest. Excess costs incurred due to force majeure, written direction by PPC, and retroactive increases to scale personnel under collective-bargaining agreements are excluded from overbudget computation.

Possibly due to a lack of understanding of the English language, the above provision has generated some disagreement. Most accountants would interpret the provision to mean that if the cost of production exceeds the approved budget by the lower of $300,000 or 10% of the budget, then all costs in excess of the budgeted amount should be added again (included twice) in computing the negative cost for net profit calculations.

The contrary interpretation would be that only those costs over budget in excess of $300,000 or 10% of the budget, whichever is lower, should be included twice in computing the negative cost for net profit calculations.

The MGM Exhibit "A" (Net Profits) contains more precise wording in Paragraph 4:

> In the event the final negative cost of the photoplay exceeds the budgeted negative cost by more than five percent (5%) of such budgeted cost, then for the purposes of this Paragraph 4, there shall be added to the final negative cost an amount equal to the amount by which the final negative cost exceeds the budgeted negative cost.

Any cost increase dictated by the studio or distributor increases in negotiated labor rates, or for any other reason outside the control of the producer (director), should be well documented so that a demand can be made for their exclusion in computing net profits.

Also, any participant other than a producer or a director (e.g., an actor or a writer) will want to make sure that this penalty provision does not apply to them and that *it was not included in their accounting by error*. Exclusion of this item is a "gimme" in negotiations for an actor or writer, but "if you don't ask, you don't get."

CROSS-COLLATERALIZATION

This term was discussed in connection with markets under Gross Receipts and in connection with Financing. The use of the same term here, in participations, refers to cross-collateralization of *pictures* and not of *markets*. So don't be confused (and if you are, do not admit it).

Many multi-picture producer deals require cross-collateralization. This simply means that the producer shares in the profits of one picture only to the extent that they exceed the losses of another designated (i.e., cross-collateralized) picture.

As an illustration, assume a producer is entitled to 50% of the net profits of pictures "A" and "B", which are cross-collateralized:

| | PICTURES | |
	"A"	"B"
Receipts	$30,000,000	$75,000,000
Distribution Fee @ 35%	10,500,000	26,250,000
Distribution Expenses	8,000,000	20,000,000
Production Cost & Interest	15,500,000	15,750,000
Total	34,000,000	62,000,000
Profit (Loss)	$(4,000,000)	**$13,000,000**
Transfer Loss From "A" to Offset Profit From "B"	4,000,000	(4,000,000)
"A" and "B" Combined	$0	$9,000,000
Producer's 50% Share		**$4,500,000**

A cross-collateralization deal can get much more complicated than this simple example. For instance, 50% of one picture might be cross-collateralized with 25% of another picture, etc.

If the first picture in a cross-collateralization deal has been distributed and results in a profit, none of this profit might be credited to the producer's share until the second picture is produced and distributed. Also, if the first picture is distributed and results in a loss (negative cost is not recouped), interest will continue to be calculated and added to the loss against any potential profits from the second picture.

The lesson here is, if you have to accept cross-collateralization as part of your deal, try to make sure that only your own films are cross-collateralized, or you could be penalized for someone else's bad luck.

RENEGOTIATION

Once upon a time, a director named George Lucas had a contract with 20th Century Fox for a film. One day, the director had a hit film called *American Graffiti*. Suddenly, the director had more clout, and his old contract seemed a tad restrictive for his newly elevated status.

According to Dale Pollock in *Skywalking*,[3] the success of *American Graffiti* gave George Lucas the opportunity to renegotiate his contract with 20th Century Fox for his new movie *Star Wars*.

Lucas's agent suggested that it might be possible to increase the producer/director's salary five-fold, to $500,000 from $100,000, and get a "gross" participation rather than participation in "net profits."

---

[3] (1983 & 1990), Samuel French Trade.

Mr. Lucas understood Hollywood dealmaking far better than most would have supposed. Instead of playing by Hollywood's rules, he wanted to set his own. So, he asked for, and got:

(1) Complete creative control, in that the movie was to be produced by his own company.

(2) Control of merchandising and a direct portion of its profits (i.e., computed separately from any net profits computations).

(3) Publishing rights to the novelization and any other books inspired by *Star Wars*.

(4) Music rights and the income from the soundtrack album (again, separated from the net profits computation).

(5) And sequel rights to any additional *Star Wars* movies.

The result of that renegotiation is today's Lucasfilm empire.

Renegotiation is common in the motion picture industry. Remember the "subject to review" discussion in connection with the sharing of box-office receipts by exhibitors and distributors?

Frequently, a network contract for an episodic series may "lowball" the license fee for the first few episodes (in order to save the network money), and if the series is successful, the contract will be renegotiated.

The authors remember a renegotiation for the movie *The Sting* that occurred subsequent to its release in order to give some net profit participation to a new actor, Robert Redford.

However, there is a right way and a wrong way to renegotiate a contract.

The proper procedure, as with any dispute, is to approach the other party in a quiet and discreet manner. While this may be show business, the industry prefers that some of its business not be shown. (An exception to that rule is attorney Pierce O'Donnell, who utilized the press handily in winning advantages for his clients in the *Coming to America* litigation, and more recently in gaining concessions for the original novelist who authored *Forrest Gump*.)

CONCLUSION

Participation agreements are complex. In most cases, due to the lack of commercial success, they are also unnecessary.

However, proper understanding of the business and careful drafting of the participation agreement can be worth hundreds of thousands (if not millions) of dollars when a motion picture *is* a commercial success. So negotiating agreements isn't something that should be done casually.

With computerized spreadsheets and other computer modeling techniques available on almost every business desktop, it behooves any producer or financier (or distributor or studio) to forecast the financial "what ifs" during the negotiation of any participation agreement. Regardless of distribution results, those negotiating deals should plan and be prepared. There should be no surprises.

Including an experienced attorney and a knowledgeable accountant during initial contract negotiations can head off problems later on. Too often, on too many major theatrical motion pictures, a financier or participant is unhappily surprised by the actual financial results. A few thousand dollars invested up front in professionals familiar with the industry can eliminate any financial surprises.

Chapter Eight

FINANCING AND INTEREST

FADE IN:

INT. CENTURY CITY TALENT AGENCY — DAY

We're back in Victoria's office. She is
reading each word from a report she is
holding tightly between two hands. Her
knuckles are white and her lips a tight,
penciled line.

Her expressions changes and she turns the
page. She looks perplexed, looking back
at the first page as if to assure herself
there is no mistake. She finishes reading,

places the paper neatly on her leather
desktop. Victoria's face bears the mark of
well-controlled astonishment.

> VICTORIA
> So, this is your recommendation?

Bernie nods, smiling slightly.

> SHARON
> I think it's brilliant! We should
> do it now!

> VICTORIA
> You do realize they aren't going to
> just roll over?

> SHARON
> What are they going to do? My
> contract says I have the absolute
> right to finance production on
> Power Lunch. It doesn't say when.
> Bernie says the way the contract
> is written I can loan the studio
> the $20 million now, and they have
> to pay me interest as if I loaned
> it two years ago when production
> started. At current rates, that's
> means they owe me about $6 million,
> plus, just on this picture. And
> since I have a three-picture deal,
> I can make the same risk-free loan
> two more times.
> (MORE)

                    SHARON (cont'd)
               (beaming)
          Is this a great country, or what?

                    BERNIE
          I can't explain why the contract
          reads that way, but it does.

                    VICTORIA
          A drafting error, maybe? I don't
          suppose it matters. I had our
          lawyers review it. They agree with
          you, Bernie. Ms. Seduction either
          has the world's best loan deal or
          grounds for a terrific lawsuit.

                    SHARON
               (sweetly)
          I do hope we can clear this up by
          next week. I am supposed to start
          filming the week after, and this
          has all got me so upset that,
          well, I just don't know how it
          will affect me.

                    VICTORIA
          (smiling tightly)
               We certainly don't want that.
               Bernie, thanks for the leverage.
               I'll make the call.

                              FADE OUT

There's no fixed formula for financing films. The methods of financing a motion picture are limited only by the imagination of the producer or financier. Or, in other words, conservative bankers need not apply.

Tales abound of creative film finance. Go to the Walt Disney Studio lot, and you'll see that the main administrative building has seven dwarves holding up the roof. The reason is, Walt Disney bet everything he had, which included mortgaging his home, to complete *Snow White*. Had the movie flopped, there would most likely not be a Walt Disney Company today, and the Disney home would have gone to the bank. So the dwarves stand as testament to the notion that a single film can support an entire motion picture company.

The motion picture business, analyst Art Murphy is fond of saying, is a "gusher business." When the well comes in, cash flows in an abundance rarely seen in any other industry.

That reality has a way of convincing people that they should take financing risks far beyond what would seem insane in other industries. Mortgaging expensive homes is a time-honored technique, though the California real-estate market crash has depleted this financing source. From time to time, a story will surface about a producer financing a film using credit cards. Generally the story is told in conjunction with a success; who knows how many projects that never pan out are floated on Visa cards?

The authors are familiar with one film that was financed by using a product advertising budget. Several major theatrical motion pictures have been financed by religious groups, the most notable in recent history being the expensive epic *Inchon*, financed entirely by Rev. Sun Myung Moon's Unification Church.

It is beyond the scope of a book on motion picture profit distribution to discuss at any length the various methods of movie financing. Even so, how a film project is financed will invariably affect participations, so it is worth discussing the most common financing methods for background purposes.

SEPARATION AND SALE OF RIGHTS

One of the most common methods of partial, if not total, financing is the separation and sale of rights. The notion is that various rights can be sold in advance to specific end users and distributors for cash. The cash, in turn, goes to producing the film.

BORROWING AGAINST PRE-SALE CONTRACTS

Many independent producers will attempt to pre-sell certain rights, usually in foreign territories. Some banks, in turn, will loan production funds secured by those pre-sale contracts, assuming they represent commitments from reputable and liquid offshore buyers.

Usually, some other security or collateral is required in addition to the pre-sale contract, because a bank generally likes to have two or three different ways in which its loan might be repaid. But in a pre-sale financing arrangement, the contract itself is the key.

Even where the contract is from a gold-plated buyer such as Canal Plus in France or Bertelsmann in Germany, the amount a bank will lend on a pre-sale contract is always a discount from face value. Consider this language from a bank commitment letter:

Loans shall not exceed 95% of the discounted present value to Borrower of executed agreements, in form satisfactory to Bank (agreements in form generally accepted for discounting by major U.S. banks in motion picture financing will be accepted by Bank), for the distribution or exhibition of (i) completed and delivered motion pictures, and (ii) uncompleted motion pictures for which the loans involved are to be used. That percentage shall be applied to a sum ("Borrower's Share") equal to the aggregate present value of such agreements net of fee, commissions, expense, reimbursements, and other sums payable to third parties and net of advances due and payable to Borrower upon execution, discounted (from due date to computation date) as follows: Contractual payments due within 1 year or less shall be discounted at Bank's then-prevailing rate on one-year certificates of deposit; those due in from 1 to 2 years at Bank's then-current prime rate; and those due in more than 2 years at the then-applicable interest rate on loans hereunder. If a payment is due upon the occurrence of an event other than the passage of a specified period of time (e.g., upon delivery of a motion picture), then a due date predicted by Bank, in its sole discretion by reasonable, good faith judgment, shall be used in determining the discount rate. The proceeds of those agreements must be pledged to Bank as provided in Paragraph 7 below. Payments under such agreements will be included in the borrowing base, as discounted hereunder, only to the extent guaranteed by letters of credit from, or confirmed by, banking institutions acceptable to Bank, in form satisfactory to Bank (unless, in its absolute discretion, Bank waives this requirement in the case of other acceptable payors). Notwithstanding the amount of the borrowing base, in no event shall the aggregate of all advances made for use in connection with a given motion picture exceed the otherwise unfinanced portion of the budgeted direct cost of that motion picture.

A distribution contract with an unknown (or even a known) distributor in many Third World countries and/or a letter of credit from Banca Primera de Timbuktu is probably not acceptable to the bank! The only way to solve this is to work very closely with the banker and the sales personnel in order to make sure the bank gets the kind of paperwork from an acceptable third party (distributor and/or bank) that says the kinds of things the bank wants to hear.

LIMITED PARTNERSHIPS

In the early 1980s, limited partnerships were in vogue for financing films. The glamour of investing in the motion picture business attracted a fair amount of private capital into various independent film projects. Even some major studios, such as Disney with its successful Silver Screen Partners and Columbia TriStar with Delphi Partners, resorted to this financing method in the late 1980s.

However, many limited partnerships proved poor investments. After the tax laws changed to eliminate the tax advantages that limited partnerships had offered, they all but disappeared from the market. But things have a way of going full cycle in the film business, and today there are again rumblings in the marketplace from individuals who would like nothing better than to create new limited-partnership vehicles for financing films.

Today, limited partnerships remain a viable means of raising capital, though they are not as easily promoted as in the halcyon 1970s and early 1980s.

When it works, a limited partnership is a very efficient format for raising the capital necessary for motion picture production and distribution. A stellar example is the Silver Screen Partners series. The first Silver Screen Partners was sold by prospectus in 1983. At that time, the partnership did not have a theatrical distribution deal in hand, though it had pre-sold certain rights to Home Box Office. The partnership eventually financed a significant number of films released through Disney. In turn, the limited partners, i.e., the investors, became profit participants in partnership projects.

Delphi was another limited partnership for the financing of theatrical motion pictures, which was quite successful in the early 1980s. The Delphi Film Associates III limited partnership was quite complicated due to the joint venture with TriStar Pictures (which at that time was itself a joint venture among CBS, Inc., CPI Film Holdings, Inc., and HBO Film Holdings, Inc., and Columbia Pictures Industries, Inc.).

After a long hiatus, several new limited partnerships have entered the marketplace, allowing Disney, Warner, and Paramount to utilize off-balance-sheet financing to help finance their production pipeline.

COMMON STOCK

The majors are huge, vertically integrated, corporate entities that are well-suited to tap the public-equity markets for cash. The same can't necessarily be said of the smaller independent film firms. Not everybody remembers this fact, however, and learning the lesson is often financially painful.

From time to time, Wall Street falls in love with Hollywood, and the public-equity markets welcome the film industry into their bosoms. Invariably, the end result is too many dollars chasing too few good films, too many bad films losing too much money, and then the inevitable disillusionment, separation, and Wall Street swearing "never again" . . . never, that is, until the memory fades and the cycle begins anew.

The most recent up-cycle in the film industry's periodic raid on the equity markets took place in the 1980s, when a large number of small production companies "went public" by selling shares of common stock. Pay-TV, home video, and foreign markets, so the pitch went, took the risk out of the business. Numerous bulletproof business plans made the rounds. Cannon Films, De Laurentiis Entertainment Group, New World Entertainment, and many others tapped the equity markets by selling common stock. The proceeds were to be used to finance the production of theatrical motion pictures.

Wall Street was in love with Hollywood; Hollywood, as always, was more than willing to accept capital from Wall Street. Unfortunately, most of these deals did not work out well for the investors. Maybe the investors did not read the "risk factors" portion of the prospectuses, such as the following in a prospectus for De Laurentiis Entertainment Group:

> Limited Operating History and Insufficient Fixed Charge Coverage: Although Mr. De Laurentiis and the management of the Company have had extensive experience in the motion picture industry, the Company is a new entity and has a limited history of operations of its own on which an investor could base an evaluation of an investment in the Company. . . .
>
> The Company was incorporated in October 1985 and over the seven months ended February 28, 1986, had a net loss of $1,515,000. Accordingly, the Company has not had sufficient earnings to cover the interest charges on the Notes offered hereby, and there can be no assurance that the Company will be able to generate sufficient income to pay such interest.[1]

---

[1] Page 6 of Preliminary Prospectus dated April 23, 1986, of De Laurentiis Entertainment Group, Inc., offering 1,500,000 shares of common stock and $45,000,000 of senior subordinated notes by Paine Webber Incorporated. The offering was a success for the underwriters; DEG did not survive into the '90s.

Or, consider this excerpt from a Kings Road prospectus:

Motion Picture Industry: Substantially all of the Company's income is derived from the distribution of its motion pictures. The motion picture industry is highly speculative and involves a substantial degree of risk. Since each picture is an individual artistic work and its commercial success is primarily determined by audience reaction (which is volatile and unpredictable), there can be no assurance as to the economic success of any motion picture. The value of a picture in the free- and pay-TV, home video, and other ancillary markets is usually dependent upon its success in the theatrical market. . . .[2]

Then there was Odyssey Filmpartners' caution to investors:

Competition; High Risk of Loss: The various aspects of the motion picture industry are highly competitive and involve a high degree of risk. The Company will be competing with major motion picture studios and numerous independent production companies with successful operating histories and greater financial and personnel resources available to them.

The market appeal and profitability of any particular motion picture or any group of motion pictures is wholly unpredictable. Audience acceptance of a motion picture represents a response not only to the film's artistic components, including the quality of the screenplay, acting, directing, and photography, but also to intangible factors which filmmakers are unable to define or predict. Investments in motion pictures have historically involved a very high degree of risk.

---

[2] Page 4 of the prospectus dated September 11, 1985, of Kings Road Entertainment offering 1,500,000 shares of common stock by Furman, Selz, Mager, Dietz & Birney, Incorporated, and Wedbush, Noble, Cooke, Inc. The company survives, but regularly posts losses.

The revenues from each picture will also depend on a number of other factors, including the ability of the distributor to place the film in desirable theaters, the timing of the release of the motion picture, the popularity of other pictures then being distributed, the reviews of film critics, the availability of alternative forms of entertainment and leisure-time activities, and the public taste generally, all of which change rapidly and cannot be predicted. There can be no assurance that the Company will realize a profit on any film in which it participates, by way of investment, production, or distribution.[3]

Many of the major independents that thrived in the 1980s—Carolco, De Laurentiis Entertainment Group Inc., The Cannon Group, Inc., Kings Road Entertainment, Management Company Entertainment Group, Inc., New Century Entertainment Corporation, New World Pictures, and Odyssey Filmpartners Ltd.—are either in bankruptcy, out of business, struggling, or have radically changed their business plans to survive.

---

[3] Page 7-8 of July 21, 1987, prospectus, Odyssey Filmpartners Ltd.

INTEREST

Most agreements between the studio/financier/distributor and the producer or other outside participant provide for an interest charge on the unrecouped investment in production cost. If the interest charge is not the actual amount based upon the actual production loan, it may be computed based upon a negotiated contractual rate. The most common rates are 125% of prime, or prime plus 1½%.

Often, this will be the same or a little more than the financier's cost of borrowing would be. The contract may state that the interest will be computed on the unrecouped balance at the prime rate of the financier's principal bank (or specify which bank) plus some points.

Participants with major studio/financiers, which must publish their actual borrowing rates in annual reports to stockholders, often claim this extra factor is a rip-off. However, what they are neglecting to take into consideration are the many costs of a loan in addition to the rate of interest (e.g., origination fees, restrictive covenants, compensating balances, etc.). In addition, the bank loan of the major studio/financier has recourse to various collateral, where the sole source of repayment for production financing is the distribution results of the motion picture.

The interest charge is computed from the first dollar spent until the production cost, including interest and, sometimes, participations in gross receipts, have been recouped. Some studio/

distributors will claim (based upon a contractual provision) that interest starts when an expenditure is accrued and monies are set aside for its payment, which may occur 30 to 90 days before the actual payment is made. Although payments during production are usually made weekly, some financier/accounting practices might compute interest from the beginning of the month in which the actual payment was made and thereby increase the interest charge. Conversely, these same accounting practices might record receipts on the last day of the month or quarter. Most accounting practices compute interest on a 360-day year, which is consistent with the method used by financial institutions.

The producer would do well to understand these and their potential impact on his participation. If appropriate, these accounting practices and procedures can become part of the up-front negotiations and amended to the producer's benefit through contractual provisions.

CHAPTER NINE

THE AUDIT

Since most of us were brought up in a world where bookkeeping is a simple matter of double-entry and don't let the hired help sign checks willy-nilly, we tend to view suspiciously any business where "creative accounting" is a norm and multiple sets of books are a business requirement.

Now, far be it from the authors to discourage you from regarding the motion picture industry with a jaded eye. But if there is blame to be had, we'd like you to focus your attention on the blameworthy.

Long after your deal is cut and closed and the picture is shot, cut, opened, and boffo, you (or your client) will receive a profit participation statement in the mail. Chances are that it will look quite similar to the statement that set Sharon Seduction off in Chapter 1, though, of course, the numbers will be different.

It may be that your picture didn't do great, in which case you are likely to toss your statement into the round file. But even if your picture cleaned up at the box office, there is a decent chance that your profit statement still won't report what you believe is your fair due.

Enter the auditor.

THE PROFIT STATEMENT

To understand what a profit participation auditor does, we first need to examine precisely what a profit statement is.

Profit participation statements represent an accounting in accordance with contractual requirements. Or, in simple terms, profit statements are creatures of contract.

The items tracked, the numbers reported, are all defined in the participations definitions that are generally attached as Exhibit "A" to the talent employment contract. Participations definitions are excruciatingly detailed contractual documents that are the foundation for the dramatically arcane world we know of as Hollywood accounting. Perhaps to better understand what profit definitions are, we should first discuss what they are not.

SOP2 IS YOUR FRIEND (NOT!)

Motion picture and television profit definitions stand in stark contrast to the financial reporting requirements promulgated by the American Institute of Certified Public Accountants as SOP 00-2 ("SOP2") Accounting by Producers or Distributors of Films.

SOP2 represents the "Generally Accepted Accounting Principles" (GAAP) applicable to the motion picture industry. The standard provides guidance to producers and distributors as to how they must prepare financial statements that the public will rely upon to judge business performance.

The SOP2 standard requires that reporting be done using the gross-profit method to amortize capitalized film costs. In plain English, that means SOP2 specifies how the accounting department is supposed to book profits and losses experienced by whatever company is exploiting any given film.

Under the gross-profit method, all costs incurred while producing a motion picture or television show are recorded on the producing entity's books as "capital expenses" reflecting the cost of creating and exploiting the project. Those "capitalized costs" include everything spent on making the picture, from development expenses to production expenditures. Those costs incurred must, in turn, be written off in direct proportion to the ultimate revenues that are generated by the project.

For example, if a film costs $30 million to produce and the distributor estimates it will generate $60 million in revenue from all sources during its entire useful life, then every time the distributor receives $1 in revenue, it must amortize $0.50 in capitalized costs.

At the end of each accounting year, the current year's revenue divided by the current and future expected revenue is multiplied by the unamortized production cost. The resulting amount is the current year's amortization. As estimates of ultimate revenues change over the life of the picture, so is the unamortized cost fraction adjusted.

SOP2 also provides for the concept of "net realizable value." This rule requires that the unamortized production cost never exceed the ultimate revenues left to come. If it does, the cost must be written down to the remaining revenue, which is known as the net realizable value. For example, if a picture is left with an unamortized production cost of $10 million, and projections show that the most it will ever generate in future revenue is $2 million, then the unamortized cost must be written down to $2 million. The $8 million write-down will appear as a loss on the books.

An interesting side-effect of the SOP2 standard is demonstrated by the way it has been abused in the past by companies wishing to maximize their financial strength, at least on paper.

The paradigm example was Cannon Films, one of the major independents in the boom days of the late 1980s. Cannon specialized in producing low-to-medium-budget pictures in volume. It was a major proponent of raising production cash by pre-selling foreign rights and borrowing against its expectations from huge credit facilities primarily funded by the French national bank, Credit Lyonnais.

Cannon is also remembered for habitually estimating revenue for their pictures far in excess of what the films ever actually earned. As a result, the company was free to amortize a fraction of the production costs compared to what would have been the case had they been more conservative in their reporting. In the short term, the result was an ability to report tremendous profits, which in turn helped keep the company's stock price at high levels.

Eventually, reality caught up with Cannon, both in the form of a more sophisticated Wall Street and an enforcement action by the Securities and Exchange Commission that was settled when the company agreed not to be so aggressive with its accounting methods. Once Cannon began amortizing its costs in a more conventional manner, huge profits turned into crushing losses. The company no longer exists, and its demise is often pointed to as one of the events that signaled the end of the go-go '80's independent film scene.

The Cannon model provides a classic example of how SOP2 allows for a reporting entity to manipulate financial information. By inflating ultimate revenue estimates, the distributor can slow down the rate of amortization, thereby increasing the profitability of the company.

For instance, our prior example of a $30 million picture with $60 million in ultimates generated $30 million in revenue this year, we would write off $15 million in cost. The transactional income statement would show a $15 million profit. If the ultimate revenues were projected at $90 million, however, the same $30 million in revenue would generate $10 million in cost amortization, resulting in a $20 million profit.

This profit, presented on the financial statements of the distributing entity, bears no relationship to contractual profits provided by profit participation agreements. Although the gross receipts and distribution expenses are the same for both types of accounting, the participation agreement's contractual provisions detailing how profits are calculated are very different from how a distributor reports profits and losses on a profit-and-loss statement.

AUDITS

TO ERR IS HOLLYWOOD

When a film is a box-office hit, profit participants generally don't trust the good graces of the distributor to ensure that their interests are being looked after. History tells us that when distributors err in calculating whether a participant is due additional compensation under a profit participation agreement, the error usually favors the distributor, not the participant. Hence, the need for participation audits and auditors.

Participation audits are a normal and expected part of the relationship between the participant and distributor. Each participation agreement contains a provision for audit rights. Auditing is not looked upon as a sign of mistrust, but a chance to confirm the propriety of the accountings and raise any issues of interpretation or equity that are not clear within the contract.

The process itself is relatively straightforward. Once the participant receives a statement from the distributor, he or she may demand an audit within a limited period of time, usually between 18 and 36 months. An auditor is then recruited from one of the small handful of firms specializing in participation audits.

When the audit is complete, the auditor provides a report to the client detailing what types of claims, if any, might be made against the distributor for additional contingent compensation. Usually the auditor will also be involved in meetings with the distributor and the participant's financial and/or legal advisors to attempt to resolve the claims informally. Most claims settle without litigation, and where a lawsuit is filed, most suits settle before trial. However, without an audit, the participant is always at a disadvantage, because the studio controls what each profit participation statement contains.

IDENTIFYING MECHANICAL ERRORS

Three types of audit claims can result from a review of profit participation statements. The first results from errors in recording information. These are simple mechanical accounting errors, though, interestingly, when these types of errors are discovered, they generally favor the distributor. The reason for this is probably related to the human tendency to take more care with an employer's interests than a stranger's.

Recording errors are also generally fairly straightforward. Expenses are often coded to the wrong picture, revenues applied improperly, or contractual nuances that differ from the standard contract language are benignly ignored by the reporting entity. Such mistakes are generally deemed "Errors Agreed To Be Corrected" in the audit report and are quickly adjusted on the participation statements.

CONTRACT INTERPRETATION

The second type of claim relates to matters of contract interpretation or ambiguity in contract language. For example, most participation contracts provide for "interest to be calculated at 125% of the prime rate on unrecouped production cost." This rather simple language does not take into account the myriad ways in which interest could be calculated.

In calculating interest for a quarterly reporting period, some distributors attempt to average the expenses of the quarter and the revenue received in the quarter; a fair and reasonable method. Other distributors assume that all costs were incurred on the forty-fifth day of the quarter while revenue was received on the ninetieth day. Such a one-sided approach opens all contractual interpretations by the latter studio to claims of overreaching.

If it hasn't been gleaned from earlier portions of this book, now is as good a time as any to stress the point that the motion picture industry has a great lack of precise definition or consistent usage of terms. Many contractual provisions utilize the definition "as that term is generally understood in the motion picture industry."

However, be aware: TERMS ARE GENERALLY UNDERSTOOD IN THE MOTION PICTURE INDUSTRY! In the authors' experience, the "generally understood" phrase works its way into a contract simply because the parties either don't want to spend the time defining terms of art or they couldn't agree on what they meant in the first place.

Because industry terms vary from distributor to distributor and from one geographic location to the next, such contractual provisions are invitations to dispute and litigation. The industry doesn't seem to care, and "generally understood" remains an important ingredient in the modern motion picture agreement.

FAIRNESS AND EQUITY

The third type of audit claim is one of fairness and equity. While some might feel that equity does not have a place within contractual relationships, the intent of an agreement is not always reflected in its language. For example, most participation agreements provide for the deduction of "direct out-of-pocket" distribution expenses. In detailing such expenses within the contract, specific mention is made of foreign remittance taxes.

Most agreements go on to note that the deductibility of such taxes will not be diminished by any manner in which the distributor treats such taxes for purposes of filing its income tax returns.

In reality, such remittance taxes are not a direct out-of-pocket cost for most distributors. They are available to be taken as a foreign tax credit on the distributor's U.S. income tax return. Even though there is explicit license in the contract for the deduction of these taxes, the expense charge does not seem to be equitably within the spirit of the agreement.

CLAIMS

After the books and records of the distributor have been reviewed (to the extent these records have been made available to the auditor), a report is prepared for the client listing the procedures performed; claims or issues discovered; and other comments that the client may find useful, such as listings of package allocations in domestic and foreign television sales. This report is submitted to the distributor and a series of negotiations normally follow.

Although each claim is discussed individually, no single claim, other than errors that have been agreed to, is ever settled. No distributor wants to set a precedent for other participants and future audits. A flat payment, referred to in a general release and settlement that acknowledges no wrongdoing on the part of either party, resolves all issues raised in the audit.

VERTICAL INTEGRATION

As noted in Chapter 3, the Paramount Consent Decree forced the major distributors to divest their theater holdings and limit their business to motion picture and television production and distribution. As government intervention has declined, vertical integration has made its way back into the entertainment business. In an attempt to create synergy at every level in the distribution and exhibition process, the studios have merged with or purchased complementary businesses in order to control every dollar in the entertainment process:

Disney owns ABC and Miramax Films

20th Century Fox owns Fox Broadcasting Company and numerous local affiliated stations (Fox O&Os)

Paramount's parent company, Viacom, also owns CBS and Showtime.

Warner Bros. parent, Time Warner, has the WB Network of affiliated local stations, New Line Pictures, Turner Entertainment and HBO.

Universal recently merged with NBC.

Sony is the only major without a network television affiliation but participated in the purchase of MGM and United Artists with an investment group.

The possibilities for cross-promotion are endless. Take, for example, a hypothetical television series developed at Disney. Disney could license the series to ABC, negotiating the network license fee with itself. The rooms of the children starring in the series could display countless Disney classic characters as props.

The show could be sold in barter syndication, including ABC-owned and -operated stations or Disney-owned local television stations with Disney setting up an ad hoc network and selling its barter retained spots. These spots could be purchased by Walt Disney Pictures to advertise its feature films; by Disneyland; or by ABC to advertise its other shows.

These relationships have spawned a new flurry of vertical-integration litigation that will continue as the studios expand their influence. The issue can be addressed as part of contract negotiations, but the standard studio agreement presumes arm's length transactions and puts the burden on the participant to prove otherwise.

The best a participations auditor can do is raise awareness of the relationships and issues as part of any audit report so that the question can be addressed as part of an audit settlement.

If the parties cannot come to terms, litigation may follow. Although this is a last resort, it is the only remaining avenue open to the participant. Historically, such cases are resolved during the discovery process. It is the rare participation audit that gets its day in court.

CHAPTER TEN

NEGOTIATING FROM POWER

FADE IN:

INT. MAJOR STUDIO CHAIRMAN'S OFFICE — DAY

The CHAIRMAN paces in front of his floor-to-ceiling picture window overlooking the 500-acre main studio lot. The PRESIDENT is seated in a finely appointed antique chair before the Chairman's expansive hand-built mahogany desk. Two vice-presidents hover silently in the background, fearing that they might be noticed, terrified they will never be acknowledged.

                    CHAIRMAN
          It's ludicrous! No court would ever
          enforce her contract that way!

                    PRESIDENT
                 (evenly)
          We've had the document reviewed by
          legal affairs. They say there is
          some danger. The courts aren't what
          worry them. It's the juries.

The chairman stops pacing and turns squarely
toward the three senior executives. He glares
challengingly.

                    CHAIRMAN
          What happens if we tell them to get
          lost?

                    PRESIDENT
          You know better than me. Victoria
          and you go way back.

The chairman looks down, thoughtfully.

                    CHAIRMAN
          Yes, Victoria will go to war, and
          her wars are always bloody. But
          she's not the one I'm worried
          about.

                    PRESIDENT
          I've made other pictures with Ms.
          Seduction. She is one tough woman.
          She's also walking, talking

box-office, and she's supposed to
walk and talk in our $150 million
summer film beginning in about a
week and a half.
          (he leans back casually
          in his chair)
Like to gamble?

The chairman smiles tightly, looking up and
over the rim of his glasses.

                    CHAIRMAN
          I do. But not with my major summer
          release.

He turns his back on the others to once
again gaze through the glass on his film
empire below.

                    CHAIRMAN
          Make the deal.

                                        FADE OUT

Ultimately, every relationship in Hollywood is defined by power.

To some extent, that power is defined by track record. When negotiating a typical producer deal with a major studio, for example, the studio's negotiator always asks what the producer has done in the past, and how much they got on their *last* deal, before agreeing to the terms of the new bargain. Indeed, it isn't unusual for a studio attorney to call a competitor to verify the producer's "quotes." Antitrust implications aside, the lesson is, what you have accomplished in the past plays a direct role in what you can negotiate for the future.

Where contingent compensation is involved, power can also come from knowledge.

For example, the standard writer's backend in a theatrical film deal presently falls at around 5% of the net. But a net player is always in a less advantageous position than a gross player, for all of the reasons described earlier in this book.

An uninformed negotiator might mistakenly agree to 5% of the producer's share of the net, which translates to a fraction of the standard deal, since it is only a fraction of the fraction the producer is entitled to. A more knowledgeable representative will insist on 5% of the entire net, and ask for a definition no less favorable than that provided the producer. In this way, the writer is insured a full 5% share of 100% of the film's net profits, and is guaranteed that no matter how poor a net deal might be, this one at least will be no worse than that negotiated by the producer, who generally has more negotiating clout.

A truly aggressive writer's representative will go after an adjusted gross deal. Not every studio will give a writer adjusted gross, and every deal varies, but if you don't ask, you don't get. And while 3% of the adjusted gross is roughly equivalent to 5% of the net in dollars, when the writer's next deal comes along, there's a precedent set—this is a *gross* player we're dealing with, not a net player. The perception is that the talent is more desirable, and a new deal's terms should reflect that perception.

There are other tricks of the trade as well.

Where talent is especially confident in a project, for example, they might consciously agree to a smaller up-front fee in exchange for more of the backend. If that is the case, the studio needs to hear the message loud and clear right at the start, so that the deal terms fully reflect the talent's desires.

Or, in addition to a net or gross participation, it might be possible to negotiate bonus payments tied to some objective measure of a picture's success. One such device is a bonus paid each time a film reaches a certain amount in domestic gross as reported by either *Daily Variety* or *The Hollywood Reporter*. So, a producer might be entitled to a $100,000 bonus when the picture exceeds $60 million in domestic gross, an additional $100,000 at $80 million, etc. This sort of arrangement, while difficult to obtain, has the twin advantages of being free from the arcane nuances of profit participation definitions and being easy to verify. Again, if you don't ask, you don't get.

LEARNING THE TRICKS

Just as there are variations on the standard deal that studios will agree to, there are items that simply aren't negotiated. To make it even harder, where there is room to negotiate, the person on the other side of the deal usually won't let on what they are willing to give away. So learning the tricks of the trade is essential. It's also very difficult to do alone.

There is a perception that the studios will not negotiate changes to their standard profit participation definitions. That perception is partially correct, and partially wrong. There are some *terms* that are non-negotiable, even while other terms might be modified. For example, with very few exceptions, no studio will give more than the 20% royalty on home video. But it is not uncommon to adjust the network-television distribution fee downward, on the theory that it only takes one phone call to make that sale.

The authors are aware of several studios that have a detailed addendum, known as a "rider," to their definitions that are meant to save negotiating points that the studios are ready to give up when asked. Some have two different addendums: one good, the other better.

Those addendum aren't offered freely, but they exist. Whether or not you get one depends on whether or not you have sufficient clout and whether or not you know to ask.

When all is said and done, some general negotiating points are always good to keep in mind while setting up a deal:

GROSS VERSUS NET

Gross is generally more than net, provided the percentages are equivalent. All things being equal, if a studio offers net, ask for the equivalent in adjusted gross. Conversely, if you're a studio, try to make a net deal of a gross deal.

TYING TO A MORE POWERFUL PLAYER

For the most part, just how good a deal you can negotiate depends upon your track record, how important you are to the project, how "hot" the project is, and all those sundry other details that define what we usually refer to as "clout." But to enhance any position, always be on the lookout for ways to tie your fortunes to a more powerful participant in the project. The benefits are obvious.

Whenever possible, require that your profit participation definition be no less favorable than that granted anyone else on the project. Therefore, if Sylvester Stallone winds up starring, that is a major plus for your own deal.

Alternatively, ask that a profit participation be a minimum percentage of net/adjusted gross, etc., but *no less* than a pre-determined fraction of the star or director's backend. This is usually hard to achieve, but once you have it, there's a precedent for future deals.

CROSS-COLLATERALIZATION

If you're fortunate enough to be negotiating for multi-picture deals, make sure that the films are not cross-collateralized, that is, that the poor performance of one will diminish the strong performance of another.

WATCH THE PROJECT

Just because a film is successful at the box office doesn't mean that there will be a profit for the participant to share. Kevin Costner's *Waterworld* grossed more than $100 million at the domestic box office, a major hit by most standards. But the film cost an estimated $200 million to produce. The lesson is obvious—big box-office sometimes means big profits, and sometimes it means something else.

When making a deal, try to understand as many nuances of the project as humanly possible. Is the film a star vehicle likely to attract Jack Nicholson or Jim Carrey? Then expect that there will be a significant first-dollar gross participant on board and plan accordingly. This is the time to ask for a bonus tied to domestic box-office performance.

Calculate the project's budget, its anticipated release costs, other special attributes that might affect the participation formula. An animated children's film has merchandising possibilities that a comedy remake using stock characters probably does not. A picture with an all-star soundtrack creates the possibility of serious soundtrack revenues. Keep a look out for the strengths and the weaknesses of each project, then integrate them into the negotiations.

Sometimes, profit participations are take-it-or-leave-it propositions because of the other players involved. One major male star is infamous for requiring tough terms for all other participants on his projects, but there is a recognized tangible benefit from being in business with the star, so people are willing to make deals they wouldn't otherwise entertain.

Each project is different, and there are no magic formulas that work in every case. Be cautious.

Use a Standard Definition

When you are negotiating for a production company, always make clear that any net profits that are part of the deal are *defined profits*. Never leave this ambiguous, lest the talent come back later and claim they did not understand the deal.

A good practice is to refer to contingent compensation as "defined net proceeds" or "defined gross proceeds," abandoning the term "profits" altogether. It's also useful to incorporate the distributor's definition into your deals whenever possible, or, if not, then to specify that the definition of "defined proceeds" is the one used by whatever distributor picks up the project.

Where a production company is selling off rights on its own, it may wish to adopt a definition from a favorite distributor, make a few changes to personalize the document, and then utilize it in every deal. But the underlying principal still applies—always make sure it is absolutely clear that a definition applies.

STANDARD RIDERS AND MODIFICATIONS

If you are negotiating for talent, ask if there is a standard rider for the profit definition and try to get it. Take care—sometimes studios maintain multiple riders, so make sure the one you get has the preferred terms.

If you are negotiating for a production company, standard riders can be good things. A production company can offer talent either good-faith negotiation or a standard rider, while indicating that the final deal will never be better than what the rider provides. This has the advantage of cutting down negotiating time, but still leaving talent with the feeling that they came away with the best possible deal.

DEFINING THE ISSUES

When negotiating any definition, it is in the talent's best interests to attempt to negotiate every identifiable issue, while the production company or studio would prefer to limit such negotiations as much as possible.

Cross-collateralization, overbudget penalties, direct accounting in certain foreign territories, checking and collection, and advertising overhead are common areas for negotiation. Distribution fees, home video shares, and interest charges are uncommon areas. Both sides need to be reasonable in setting the deal, but it is useful to attempt to set parameters on negotiations early on. This is usually accomplished by the talent requesting everything they can think of, and the studio/production company explaining what it will discuss and what is never negotiated.

If you are established talent, chances are you will want to retain experienced transactional counsel and/or a talent agent to negotiate your deal for you. If you can't afford a lawyer and don't have an agent, read the contracts closely and ask for more cash up front.

CONCLUSION

Contingent compensation is a hot topic in the modern motion-picture world. On one hand, talent is ever more insistent that it share in the fruits of its creative labor. On the other side, studios and distributors want to attract the best talent, but preserve enough of the profits to compensate them for their own contributions of capital and expertise. The balance between the two sides is in constant flux, and it doesn't help matters that Hollywood has evolved a profit participation system that is so arcane even the experts are sometimes left with more questions than answers.

But contingent compensation is part of just about every film deal, and anyone who negotiates participation terms casually is putting themselves or their client at a competitive disadvantage. It is fundamental that the individual negotiating on the other side will never tell you what you've left on the table. In the case of contingent compensation, you can easily lose a valuable asset and never even know it's missing.

One of the hallmarks of a seasoned Hollywood insider is a basic understanding of how contingent compensation works, and how to negotiate a good deal. Spend some time on the subject. Your passion will likely be well-rewarded.

EXT. PACIFIC COAST HIGHWAY — DAY

A red Lamborghini races past the Malibu
Colony.

Bernie is relaxing behind the wheel, cruising
slightly ahead of the tourist traffic. The
top is down. The sun is gentle, the wind in
his face brisk and exhilarating.

> SHARON (OS)
> The studio said it was only
> fair that Sharon Seduction share
> in the success of Power Lunch
> given her critically acclaimed
> performance and unexpectedly
> strong public reception
> domestically and overseas.

> BERNIE
> See? They love you!

Wide shot of Sharon sitting in the passenger
seat, reading aloud from the Hollywood
Reporter, a copy of Daily Variety in her lap.
She is wearing fashionable sunglasses, a silk
scarf wrapped about her head to keep out the
sun and provide a modest disguise.

> SHARON
> (laughing)
> That isn't the word Victoria
> used. Anyway, thanks to you,
> my agent got them to "update" my
> (MORE)

deal and I am now a very happy first-
dollar player. Not only that, but I
told Victoria I've learned enough about
studio accounting to know that I'll
always need you. Expect a call from her
tomorrow — you and your firm are going
on permanent retainer.

                 BERNIE
          I'm flattered.

A cell phone rings. Sharon pulls a portable
unit from her bag.

                 SHARON
          Yes? Oh, that's fine. Tell them
          I'll be there by two.

Sharon pushes the button to disconnect.

                 SHARON
          That was Jennifer. She said, "Hi!"

                 BERNIE
          You realize she spends most of her time
          these days telling people how you are
          not only the most beautiful and talented
          woman in the world, you're also the
          smartest because you hired her as your
          personal assistant?

                 SHARON
          She wants to produce. I need the
          help. She's really very good. I
          don't think David is a big fan,
                    (MORE)

though. Jennifer put off the
wedding until after we're
through filming.

                    BERNIE
          Don't worry about David.
          Victoria is keeping him busy.
          I understand he's becoming the
          firm's guru on negotiating
          participation deals.

Bernie turns into a wide driveway surrounded
by an immaculately landscaped garden.
Sharon reaches into her bag; a moment later
the wrought-iron gate begins to slowly
open. Bernie's Lamborghini glides up the
driveway toward Sharon's pearl-white mansion
overlooking a pounding blue surf.

                    BERNIE
          Where would you like me to drop you?

                    SHARON
          You're not going to stay a while?

                    BERNIE
          I'd love to. But I have to be
          back in the office to go over
          some figures for a client.

                    SHARON
               (softly)
          I'm a client. I have a figure.

                              FADE TO BLACK

GLOSSARY

Following are terms commonly used in motion-picture profit participation contracts and accounting. The definitions are not exhaustive, but are meant as guides. For a term's true meaning in the context of any particular deal, pay careful attention to the underlying agreements and definitions.

Accrual Accounting An accounting method in which revenue is recognized when earned and expenses are recognized when accrued.

Actual Breakeven A point at which *Gross Receipts* equal the sum of the (1) studio distribution fees, (2) distribution expenses, (3) negative cost, (4) studio overhead charges, (5) interest charges, and (6) deferments payable at *Actual Breakeven* or from first net profits. *Actual Breakeven* is always calculated on a cash basis. It comes in various flavors, including *Initial Actual Breakeven* and *Rolling Actual Breakeven*, depending upon whether the defined "breakeven" remains fixed once it is reached or is recalculated with each successive participation statement.

Adjusted Gross Receipts *Gross Receipts* minus *Off-the-Top* deductions ("OTTs"). *Off-the-Tops* include trade dues, checking and collection fees, residuals, and taxes.

Artificial Break-Point A predetermined "breakeven" point that is arrived at without reference to actual revenues or expenditures. *The Artificial Break-Point* is arrived at by using some limited fixed criteria such as a multiple of production cost. What this does is decrease the variability of breakeven because it limits the criteria upon which breakeven is based. By contrast, *Cash Breakeven* and *Initial Actual Breakeven* are directly affected by all changes in costs, pre-break participations, etc. An *Artificial Break-Point* is utilized to provide the participant with more certainty about when breakeven is achieved.

Cash Accounting An accounting method in which revenue is recognized when cash is received and expenses are recognized when cash is disbursed.

Cash Breakeven That point in time when *Gross Receipts* equal the sum of (1) a negotiated distribution fee, (2) studio distribution expenses, (3) negative cost, (4) studio overhead, and (5) interest.

Contractual Overhead Charge A charge for overhead contained within a participation definition. Generally a percentage figure, the contractual overhead charge does not necessarily relate directly to actual overhead.

Deferment A payment that is contingent upon accomplishing some pre-agreed event, usually a defined breakeven point.

Distribution Fee The fee charged by the studio/distributor to distribute the product. Usually charged as a percentage of revenue from any given market (e.g., theatrical, television, etc.), standard distribution fees vary widely and can range from as low as 10% to as high as 50%.

First-Dollar Gross What the most powerful talent can command. It is equivalent to gross receipts minus "off-the-top" deductions, typically trade dues, checking and collection fees, taxes, and residuals.

Fixed Compensation **Against** *Contingent Compensation* A flat fee applied against eventually defined proceeds. Used in the context of talent who are entitled to fixed-dollar payments up front that will be applied against future contingent compensation. Generally, these deals apply to *First-Dollar Gross Participants* who are assured they will receive contingent compensation. The *Advance* is payable up front, and is deducted from the contingent compensation the participant is entitled to once the project begins generating revenue.

Gross Participant A participant entitled to a percentage of *Gross Receipts* less certain pre-agreed deductions. *Gross Participants* come in various flavors, including *First-Dollar Gross Participants* and *Adjusted Gross Participants*.

Gross Receipts The total revenues reported to the profit participant. This will generally not equal the total revenues actually generated by the project, since the *Home Video Royalty* usually represents only 20% of the wholesale price of home video sales.

Hard Floor Utilized where a participant's own contingent participation share is reducible by participations granted to others, the *Hard Floor* is a strict minimum percentage participation, as distinguished from a *Soft Floor*, which is only a point at which a participant and a studio will begin sharing reductions in contingent compensation as additional net-profit shares are granted to others.

Home Video Royalty In a standard deal, home video revenue is reported to the participant at the rate of 20% of the wholesale price charged by the studio. This rate is generally non-negotiable. However, A-level talent has recently been able to increase the royalty to as much as 40%.

Initial Actual Breakeven The point in time at which *Gross Receipts* equal the sum of expenses. The expenses used to offset revenues are (1) distribution fees charged by the studio, (2) the studio's distribution expenses, (3) negative cost, (4) studio overhead chargeable to negative cost, (5) interest, (6) deferments payable at *ABE* or out of the first dollar of net profits, and (7) gross participations. This concept is only important to a participant with a gross-participation position after *Initial Actual Break-even* is reached. Subsequent to this point when negative cost and studio overhead have been recouped, the gross participant will no longer bear distribution fees and non-off-the-top distribution expenses. *Initial Actual Breakeven* is the functional equivalent of net profits.

Motion Picture Association of America *MPAA* is *the* association of major film studios. Counting each of the majors as a member, the MPAA acts as Washington lobbyist, anti-piracy watchdog, industry statistician, and more for the studios.

Negative Cost The cost of creating a filmed entertainment product—literally the cost of creating the filmed product up through the completed negative.

Net Participant A participant who shares in the net profits (defined net proceeds). Also someone who wishes they had more leverage.

Net Profits (aka Net Proceeds) *Gross Receipts* less (1) studio distribution fees, (2) distribution expenses, including OTTs and advertising overhead, (3) negative cost, including gross participations paid up to *Actual Breakeven*, (4) studio overhead, (5) interest, (6) all deferments and gross participations payable. Distribution fees and distribution expenses continue to be charged each statement period. (See *Initial Actual Breakeven.*)

Off-the-Tops (OTTs) Deductions that apply when calculating a *First-Dollar Gross Participation*. These include trade dues, checking and collection fees, taxes, and residuals.

Output Deal A deal that gives a programmer exclusive rights to the output of a given supplier for a set period. For example, a five-year output deal between a studio and a pay-TV service gives the service access to each studio title released during the contract period, and precludes the studio from licensing any such title to another pay-programmer.

Rolling Actual Breakeven A defined breakeven that is recalculated with every statement to include additional distribution expenses on a continuing basis grossed up for the effect of the distribution fee.

Soft Floor Utilized where the participant's own contingent compensation share is reducible by profit shares granted to net participants, the *soft floor* is the point at which the studio begins to share in the reduction with the participant on some percentage basis. For example, a producer might be granted 17½% of the adjusted gross, reducible to a *soft floor* of 12%. Other net participations granted on the project will be borne solely by the producer until the producer's profit share is reduced to the 12% *soft floor*, after which the producer and studio will bear any further reductions on a pro-rata basis. Unless a *Hard Floor* is in place, additional net participants can theoretically reduce the producer's share to zero.

Vertical Integration When used to describe a media enterprise, vertically integrated means that the corporation owns or controls assets that participated in every aspect of its business from manufacturing through final distribution. A good example is Time Warner, Inc., which owns film and television production and distribution, cable television systems, a mini-network, a magazine empire, etc.

INDEX